PRAISE FOR *LESSONS* *DRIVE-THRU*

"*Lessons From the Drive-Thru* provides insights into more than 30 years of hands-on, frontline restaurant leadership experience – masterfully weaving in triumphs, failures, and lessons learned with Monica's trademark authenticity and perseverance. The book is filled with invaluable wisdom that anyone could apply to their leadership journey, all grounded in Monica's grit, humanity and deep commitment to growing people."

— David Gibbs, CEO of Yum! Brands, Inc.

"Monica has absolutely nailed it with this uplifting sharing of her journey. *Lessons from the Drive-Thru* is an opportunity to learn from one of the most experienced, courageous, and common-sense operators and executives that I have ever had the honor of working with. This read will inspire frontline leaders never to underestimate their influence or their ability to make a real difference in countless lives. It will challenge executives to behave in a way that is authentic, to re-think what really matters, and to lead with heart. It will cause reflection, evoke emotion, and spark action. *Read this book* – I wish I had long ago!"

— Mike Kulp, CEO of KBP Brand

"Say 'yes!' to this terrific first-person tale of growth and accomplishment. Monica shares her compelling story of taking risks that led to advancement in the restaurant industry. This book is packed with practical advice for anyone stepping up to lead for the first time!"

— Denny Marie Post, Former CEO of Red Robin

"Rothgery is the sort of leader you want to follow — in life, and on the page. This book is for anyone who leads, wants to lead, longs for better leadership, or who just plain loves a good success story."

— Laura Munson, *New York Times* and *USA Today* bestselling author, and founder of the acclaimed Haven Writing Retreat

"Monica Rothgery is the real deal. From managing a Taco Bell to becoming the COO of KFC, she has done it all. Her vast experience turns into powerful wisdom that can make you a better leader."

— Shep Hyken, customer service/CX expert and *New York Times* bestselling author

"If you're a leader, you need to read this book! Monica Rothgery brings a much-needed fresh perspective to the dusty leadership discussions we keep having. She breaks down what it takes to create and keep teams worth having and reminds all of us that, if we want to change our organization, we must first change ourselves. I trust Monica with my team – and you should with yours!"

— Gabrielle Bosché, CEO of The Purpose Company

"The lessons Monica shares go beyond sectors and geographies. Be yourself (authenticity) and start with people first (servant leadership). Results will follow. Monica lived these every single day when I worked with her in Thailand, and the recipe worked! Monica was incredibly successful in her COO roles, but also made a big difference as a chief people officer and coach to many, including me. I'm grateful she decided to share her experiences and lessons through this book with others, written in the most engaging and authentic way – just like Monica!"

— Sameer Aggarwal, CEO Asia, Cognita Schools
Former CEO of Walmart, India

"Monica Rothgery skillfully shares her journey with honesty, vulnerability, and self-reflection, resulting in a powerful manual for franchisees, managers, or anyone wanting to excel at operations. She proves that well-managed people lead to well-earned profits. Only someone who's done it could have written this incredible book."

— Scott Greenberg, Business Speaker & Author,
Stop the Shift Show and *The Wealthy Franchisee*

"Monica is one of a kind. The genuine and authentic stories that shaped her extraordinary career are life lessons not just for restaurant operators but for anyone on a leadership journey, whether in business or in life. A page-turner with raw, hilarious, and inspiring stories, this book is a must read."

— Sabina Rivi, Chief Financial Officer,
Maple Leaf Sports & Entertainment
Owner of the Toronto Maple Leafs and the Toronto Raptors

"It's not the marketers that define restaurant brands – but rather the operators. In my role as KFC Global CEO, I wanted inspirational leaders who were intellectually smart but conveyed warmth and understanding. Monica was exceptional – her leadership at KFC Thailand was so impressive that it led her to the KFC USA Operational leadership role. To succeed in such different environments requires a strong and insightful approach, deep restaurant experience, and a determination to set tough goals and deliver on them. Monica didn't miss – I strongly recommend her book as a pragmatic guide to becoming a successful leader."

— Roger Eaton, Former CEO of KFC Global

"I could feel the emotions behind each story. Leaders take these gut punches every day and we keep going. This book is for new and seasoned leaders to remember they are not alone."

— Katelyn Phillips, Restaurant Manager, Taco Bell

LESSONS
FROM THE
DRIVE-THRU

Real Life Wisdom
for Frontline Leaders

MONICA ROTHGERY

Publishing support provided by
Ignite Press
55 Shaw Avenue #204
Clovis, CA 93612
www.IgnitePress.us

ISBN: 979-8-9896765-0-7
ISBN: 979-8-9896765-2-1 (E-book)

For bulk purchases and for booking, contact:

Monica Rothgery
Monica@MonicaRothgery.com
MonicaRothgery.com

Library of Congress Control Number: 2023922802

Cover design by Usman Tariq
Edited by Lynn F. Thompson and Elizabeth Arterberry
Interior design by Jetlaunch

FIRST EDITION

Scan here or go to MonicaRothgery.com/free-guide
to download a summary and discussion guide for
Lessons from the Drive-Thru: Real Life Wisdom for Frontline Leaders.

To Lori and Onyxe
you chose me

TABLE OF CONTENTS

FOREWORD

From managing a Taco Bell restaurant to leading from the corner office at KFC, Monica Rothgery is living proof that the drive-thru can be a pathway to not just delicious tacos, but to incredible growth and fulfillment.

Monica's story isn't just about rising through the ranks; it's about finding your authentic self and using that as your secret ingredient for success. In a world where leadership often feels like a scripted recipe, she breaks the mold and shows us that being genuine is the key to making meaningful connections – whether you're serving up tacos or steering a global brand.

This book isn't your typical business guide either. It's a journey through stories – heartwarming, hilarious, and sometimes a bit messy, just like life. Through *Lessons from the Drive-Thru: Real Life Wisdom for Frontline Leaders*, she weaves together the essence of being a true servant leader – caring for your team, supporting their growth, and fostering an environment where everyone thrives. It's a lesson in humility, wrapped in a tortilla of empathy, and topped with a sprinkle of life-changing inspiration.

Lessons from the Drive-Thru demonstrates how leaders can use their position to change lives, one taco at a time.

Monica takes us behind the scenes. She highlights the challenges of being a restaurant leader while finding joy in the work.

So, if you're a new frontline manager or a seasoned leader looking for a fresh perspective, this book is your golden ticket. It's a reminder that no matter where you come from or where you're headed, your journey is your own unique blend of flavors. And just like Monica, you can turn your experiences into a recipe for success, authenticity, and change a few lives along the way.

Live Mas...

> — *Greg Creed, Former CEO of Yum! Brands,*
> *Author of* R.E.D. Marketing,
> *and advisory board member for Craveworthy Brands*

A NOTE FOR MANAGERS

Dear Manager:

That's how most letters to you begin. "Dear Manager" – and usually they are a complaint from a customer, a bill from a vendor, or an advertisement from a new floor mat cleaning company. However, this Dear Manager is a letter from me to you with a special message.

Being a manager is hard. Good team members are hard to find. Employees don't show up for their shifts. Some don't even call to let you know they aren't coming. Your assistant manager forgets to place the food order. The inventory counts are off, and you are due for your quarterly inspection. You know how to do the job. You set a plan for your week. You organize your day, but your plan is out the window by noon. The cook didn't show. Your opening manager had car trouble, and the delivery truck arrived two hours late. You manage to get through lunch rush, put away the truck order, enter the receipts, count down the drawers, and, before you know it, it's time for dinner rush. After dinner, you look at your "to-do" list and realize you did nothing. You didn't schedule the three interviews or order replacement gaskets for the walk-in cooler. You resolve to finish the schedule and read the new marketing promo material at home. That is until your closing manager calls and says she is sick.

I know because I did it. I know what it's like to worry about labor and food cost targets. I have had upset customers toss drinks at me. I had to drive to my store in the middle of the night to meet the police because the alarm went off. I know the dread of an audit, the fear of failure, and the desire to make every customer happy.

This book is about my struggles as a restaurant manager and the lessons I learned. To have a different experience, not to struggle and always be exhausted, I had to see my role differently. I had to learn about people, about teamwork, and about myself. Once I started to think and act differently, things changed – not overnight, but gradually. My turnover decreased. My team got more relaxed. I got more relaxed. Our business results improved.

I had to see my role differently. I had to learn about people, about teamwork, and about myself.

And then, the magic happened. I discovered I could help team members in ways I had never imagined.

I struggled because I thought I was alone. I was too proud or afraid to ask for help. Well, you are not alone either. You have me. You can learn from my mistakes and take a shortcut to having more fun and getting better results.

One more thing – this book is written from the perspective of a restaurant manager. Still, it is really for anyone who leads a team because the lessons are universal truths about leadership and about people. Whether you lead a restaurant, a retail store, a hotel, a rental car outlet, a call center, a line at a factory, or any other team, this book will show you, the frontline leader, how to find fulfillment in your role while you change lives.

A NOTE FOR COACHES

Dear Coach:

If you are lucky enough to coach frontline leaders, this book is also for you. Perhaps you started as a frontline leader and were promoted to an area or district or regional manager role. Now you are a coach. If that is the case, you know firsthand that being a manager is difficult. My friend Bill Ford, Vice President of Operations for Stewart Restaurant Group, says about managers, "There are a few great ones who have figured it out, but too many can't get out of their own way."

But what if you can help them get out of their own way? What if all your managers were like "the great ones who have figured it out?" Why can't they be? I suppose it could be that some are just not that talented, but I think more realistically: we haven't taught them how. We haven't shown them how to focus on the bigger picture. We haven't taught them how to spend their time on the big ideas.

Please don't hear this as criticism. You have challenging jobs, too. There is pressure to deliver results, find and train managers, build new restaurants, order equipment – your list is just as endless. So, wouldn't more all-star managers make your life easier?

This book can help. It outlines a path for you to coach your managers to find more success and more enjoyment in their role. Through your encouragement and support, the managers can learn to play bigger roles, grow your business, and change lives. The lessons outlined here are a roadmap for you to coach them to fulfillment and success.

Like the managers, you, too, may have to change how you think about your role. You may have to spend your time in different ways and take a few risks. Your routine might need to change, but isn't the possibility of a self-sufficient, thriving team of successful frontline leaders worth it?

Before we go on, let's talk about the elephant in the room: labor costs. We all know the pressure on labor is real, and it's not getting better. Margins are razor thin, and there is no room for error, but you must give your managers a little room to grow. They need time to try new skills. If they don't feel like they have your support, they won't risk trying.

You may say, "Impossible! We don't have extra labor to waste. We need the managers to be productive." Let's look at that.

What is productive? Is productive working in a position as an overpaid team member? Sure, that's necessary during lunch rush, but what about after lunch rush? What if we expand or even re-define "productive?" What if "productive" is developing the team to be more efficient? We know that efficiency can reduce mistakes, improve service, and lower labor costs. What if "productive" means building an engaging and caring culture so that turnover is cut in half and the team shows up for each other? Service and ultimately sales improves when the team is engaged and focused. What if "productive" means finding ways to blunt the new restaurant opening across the street or partnering with the high school football team on a sponsorship? A productive manager can grow their team, sales, and profit if she has time.

I hear you. Labor is tight. So, what if – to start – you gave them six minutes out of every hour? Six minutes to try something new. I am sure that you can find that time. That would accumulate to one hour per shift. What if you checked up on that one hour of productivity the same way you check up on sales, food cost, and labor? I can assure you that if you encourage them to use that one hour to be productive in a different way, you will see the results. Your business will grow. Your teams will stabilize. Your managers will relax and, most importantly, your customers will notice.

Your managers are frontline heroes. They have the power to change lives, and, in the process, grow your business. Let's show them how.

PREFACE

This story is my story as I remember it. Most of it takes place from 1992 to 1996, when I was a very young, inexperienced restaurant manager of a Taco Bell in the suburbs of Chicago. I was recruited as a high potential JMO (junior military officer) to participate in a pioneer program called "Organization of the Future." We called it OOF, sometimes GOOF. The program was designed to develop self-sufficient, self-led work teams. The theory was that if the restaurant teams were self-led, then the restaurant manager could run two, three, or even four restaurants. The program was ultimately canceled, but lessons were learned.

We learned that every restaurant needs a leader. For the following thirty years, if I ever heard a whisper of a manager running two restaurants, I would recoil and strike. Absolutely not! We also learned that a manager needs a coach to support them. In the '90s, my coach had over sixty restaurants. That doesn't happen anymore. We learned that, ideally, a coach has six to eight restaurants.

In the '90s, I thought and acted like a young manager. I was critical of Corporate and blamed them for mostly everything. My reactions were sometimes warranted and sometimes misguided. With some maturity and experience, I can now appreciate that everyone was doing their best.

In 1997, when PepsiCo spun off the restaurant brands Taco Bell, Pizza Hut, and KFC, I was an associate manager in the Training Department at Taco Bell. I listened as CEO David Novak talked about creating a new company – a restaurant company that focused on restaurants. He challenged us to build a company on core beliefs like "Build people capability first, sales and profit will follow." He espoused that the restaurant manager should be the #1 leader, and everyone else in the company is there to support the restaurant manager. The headquarters were renamed Restaurant Support Centers. This was music to my ears. Finally, the restaurant manager got to take center stage. Finally, we would do everything we could to support our frontline leader who ultimately took care of our customers. For me, it was a watershed moment. I had pledged to support the frontline leader, and now, the company was making the pledge, too.

Yum! Brands, the parent company of Taco Bell, Pizza Hut, and KFC, continually provided me with opportunities to grow my career. I worked in all three brands in both Human Resources and Operations. But, regardless of my position, my heart was always with the restaurant managers.

The greatest challenge of my career was leading Operations for KFC Thailand. I had not yet worked for KFC. I didn't know how to make fried chicken, and I did not speak Thai. The 800 restaurants had some of the lowest performance measures in the world. How could I possibly be effective as a leader?

I discovered that heart-led leadership transcends language and culture. Team members want to be seen and heard. They want training to do their jobs and opportunities to grow. They want to be included in decisions and appreciated for their work. And, they want to win! I used every leadership lesson I'd learned from when I was a restaurant manager and, together, we transformed KFC Thailand to a top-operating business. The year after I left, the team was #1 in the world in food safety!

> **Heart-led leadership transcends language and culture.**

After four amazing years in Thailand, I became the first woman to be the Chief Operations Officer (COO) for Kentucky Fried Chicken (KFC) US, leading 4,000 restaurants across the United States. I was also the first LGBTQ leader to be promoted to the Chief-level role at Yum! Brands. I hope my journey shows all leaders what is possible.

My friend and mentor, former Yum! Brands CEO Greg Creed, who graciously wrote the foreword of this book, often says, "The customer experience will never be greater than the team member's experience." I would add that the team member experience is determined by one person: the restaurant manager. My mission as COO was to provide the managers with the best tools, processes, equipment, and training so they could create a great experience for team members. Happy, engaged team members provide great guest service and make the restaurant a fun place to work. Turnover decreases. Productivity improves. Sales and profits go up. That was my simple COO formula. Everything starts and ends with the restaurant manager.

As COO, I loved visiting restaurants and meeting my KFC managers across the country. I wanted to visit the restaurants by myself so I could talk to the managers and really listen to their needs. But it never worked out that way. When I came to town, it was a circus. Everyone showed up: district managers, regional

Everything starts and ends with the restaurant manager.

managers, the franchisees, my team, even the HR people. So, I made it work. When my entourage arrived at a restaurant, I dismissed everyone else and headed straight to the restaurant manager. I insisted on a few minutes alone with them to say:

"Thank you. Thank you so much. I know how hard this job is. I know how frustrating and lonely it can be. I want you to know how proud I am of you. You are not alone, and you can do this. How can I help?"

Sometimes they cried. Often, they wanted a hug, which is hard for me because I'm not a hugger. We would take selfies and talk about what was working and not working. Mostly, I just wanted them to know that they had so much potential, so much opportunity – more than they even realized. I helped them understand that they were making their mark on their team member's lives, their communities, and their organizations.

During the COVID pandemic, fast-food managers were called "frontline heroes" because they showed up to work when many leaders were at home. They safely provided meals for doctors, nurses, emergency workers, and families stuck at home. They donated thousands of meals to hospitals and medical facilities. They were being called "heroes," and the country was recognizing something that I always knew. Like teachers and coaches, frontline leaders have the power to change the world.

Throughout my career, I have found that great leaders embrace who they are. They take care of their teams, empower others and, ultimately, change the lives of those around them. It is my sincere hope that my stories and lessons help managers become the leaders they are meant to be.

INTRODUCTION

Spring 1992. First Lieutenant, United States Army, Colorado Springs (just outside of Fort Carson)

"Hello?" I answer the rotary dial phone in my lieutenant voice, deep and authoritative.

"Monica, it's Jay. Got a minute? I want to tell you about a great opportunity in Chicago."

I wonder what it is this time. Firestone, Hallmark, and Pfizer have all passed on me. Allergan is still in play, but can I really do a skirt and heels every day to call on busy eye doctors? *Blech.*

"What's up, Jay?" I ask.

"Hear me out. Promise? Promise to hear me out?"

This is not the way I want my recruiter to start a conversation about a new opportunity. Jay's company is paid by other companies to find jobs for junior military officers, like me, who are leaving the military. They get paid lots of money to find leaders like me, and I get help finding a new job. So, it's a win-win. To date, all the potential jobs offered to me are in either manufacturing or pharmaceutical sales because of my biology degree.

"Jay, come on. I need to get to Fort Carson." As a first lieutenant, I live off base in my own apartment. It's a nice upgrade from the quonset hut in South Korea. "The company commander is having a final walk-through before we head out to the field. What is it?"

"Okay, listen. Taco Bell is doing some very interesting things—"

Taco Bell? I interrupt and laugh into the phone. "Seriously, Jay? Seriously? I went to college so I would not have to work at Taco Bell. I gotta go."

I put the phone down and go back to base. By the time I get home, I have three messages waiting.

<beep>
"Monica, it's Jay. Please call me back."
<beep>
"Monica, it's a cool opportunity to use your leadership skills and work with young people."
<beep>
"Monica, you get a free trip to Chicago and get to go to a Cubs game."

Wait, Wrigley? Okay, now I'm interested.

I call Jay back, and he explains, "Taco Bell is looking to launch a pilot program. They are recruiting young military officers, just like you, to grow into multi-unit managers, making six figures after a year or two. They believe that leading a platoon and running a restaurant, well, they are similar. Just come to Chicago and meet with them. They are taking you to a Cubs game."

A week later, I'm on a plane to Chicago to meet the Taco Bell team and hear the pitch. Funny thing – I have never been to a Taco Bell restaurant. I grew up on McDonald's and Mom's cooking. However, I had worked at Chuck E. Cheese for five years during high school and college. I had even been promoted to shift supervisor. I loved working there.

Taco Bell, hmm… Might be fun. Six figures at twenty-six wouldn't suck. Chicago is closer to the family in Cleveland. And, I need a job, like soon! I continue to muse over the possibility of a job with Taco Bell, a move to Chicago, and my May transition date as the plane sets down at O'Hare.

The VP of something or other picks me up at the airport. The van chit-chat is boring, lots of questions about the Army. *Blah, blah, blah…*

"Have you fired a gun?"

Fer god's sake… I'm in the fucking Army.

"Well, sir, we don't call them guns. We call them weapons, and, yes, I have fired a weapon. In fact, every member of the United States Army must certify in at least one weapon."

His eyes pop out of his head when I tell him that I've thrown a live grenade. Thankfully, we soon arrive at the regional office and are led to a large conference room filled with other young officers, all of whom are exiting the military and being recruited by Taco Bell.

They serve sandwiches. *Where's the Taco Bell food?* The presentation is good, really good. The video is slick, and I am enjoying meeting all of the guys. There are nearly twenty lieutenants and a few captains. I'm the only woman, which is not that dissimilar to the Army. *Someday, I won't be the only one – sigh.*

A guy named Ken explains the program. "You all are part of the future of Taco Bell. We are launching a program called Organization of the Future. This is a revolutionary way to lead restaurants and create big opportunities for big leaders. We need you to take our company into the next century. Your leadership training plus our great food and restaurants are a perfect fit.

"Our team members are like your soldiers. They are young, impressionable, and darn fun to work with. After training, you will be assigned your own Taco Bell. You are the leader. Once you hit some key performance measures, we will assign you a second restaurant, then a third and fourth. With each restaurant comes more responsibility and a bigger challenge, which we reward. Come to work with us and we will pay you a salary, plus offer you the potential to earn huge bonuses."

The numbers are eye-popping. My lieutenant pay is around $23,000 a year, and Taco Bell is starting us at $32,000 with raises when we take on more restaurants. Plus – bonuses? *This sounds interesting.*

We load up into vans and head to an actual Taco Bell. It's fun talking with the other lieutenants. We are all in the same boat: leaving the Army and heading into the unknown. Once at the Taco Bell restaurant, we meet the RGM (restaurant general manager) who proudly shows us his restaurant. In the "back-of-house," he shows us how they make the food. I immediately feel comfortable. *It is like Chuck E. Cheese, except tacos.* We wash our hands and then get to make a taco.

"This is pretty good," I say as I get my first taste of a Taco Bell taco. I scan the restaurant and do a quick Army-style assessment: *good assets, fun personnel, committed leadership, and solid money.*

We stop at the hotel for a quick change of clothes. I wander around the hotel room that I don't have to share. *This is nice! TV, big bed, coffee.* Next stop: Wrigley Field! We have great seats and enjoy beer and hot dogs. The Cubs lose, but I feel like I am winning a job, new friends, and a new home.

Two months later, on June 2, 1992, I trade my Class A uniform for a Taco Bell manager's uniform and report to my training restaurant to start my job as a Multi-Unit Restaurant Manager.

1

WASH THE DAMN
GREEN ONIONS

December 1992. Restaurant General Manager, Taco Bell, Westchester, Illinois

It's been six months since I left the Army and joined Taco Bell. I spent those months learning how to serve customers. I learned how to make tacos and burritos, take orders at the front counter and the drive-thru window, and set up the production line. I learned a lot about cleaning and a little about maintaining the facility and the equipment. I learned how to open the restaurant in the morning and how to safely close at night.

I was impressed with all the procedures and processes. I studied the procedure manual in the evening so I could recite all the standards. I memorized all the schematics to set up the line, the heated cabinets, and the refrigeration units. It was a bit like the Army. Everything had a purpose, and everything had a place. After mastering the team member positions, I learned how to run a shift. I enjoyed it like a game. Could I beat the speed-of-service goal? How fast could I close the restaurant at night?

Yes, training was fun, but it's time for reality. I am assigned my own restaurant: #4442 in Westchester, Illinois. The current manager showed me around for ten minutes and left. He is opening a new restaurant in another suburb. That was two weeks ago. Two very long weeks ago.

I am shocked by how unorganized the one-year-old restaurant is. It is under-staffed and missing sales targets. Turnover is through the roof. It's in a terrible location for a restaurant. It sits on a lot with a grocery store, but the other three sides of the lot are forest preserve. Worst of all, there is no bus service, so the team members must own cars.

I am working a lot. I have spent hours cleaning shelves, reorganizing the production line, and moving equipment to follow the company standards. We are so short-staffed that the assistant manager and I often work twelve-hour shifts. I know I need to hire and train some shift managers, but there is so much to do. So many things need my attention. The HVAC (heating, ventilation, and air-conditioning) units are not working properly, so it is hot in the kitchen. I need to call my boss to ask about the warranty. This broken equipment is only a year old! The bathroom sink leaks, and there is graffiti on the mirror. I know I have to fix all of it, but I spend most of my time serving customers because we are short-staffed. At least I have a few interviews scheduled for today.

The other thing I need to work on is the team that I do have. They do not know the standards. They don't give the proper greeting. They don't suggestive sell the promotional item when a customer is ordering. Often, they don't even say "thank you" to the customers. I assume they haven't been trained.

I arrive in the morning and take a deep breath. I resolve to start making an impact in this very broken restaurant. The key slides easily into the heavy door but the locking mechanism sticks. *Mental note – Fix door lock. How many mental notes can one mind remember?*

I enter the restaurant, and, thankfully, remember my alarm code on the first try. *Freaking security system. Hate it.* Two nights ago, the air conditioner must have blown a stray napkin in front of the motion detector and triggered the security alarm. The security company called me and the police. I drove to the restaurant at 3 am to reassure the police that the napkin was not breaking into the safe.

Once in the kitchen, I shout, "Good morning!" with forced cheerfulness.

No one replies, which is not unusual. This is a tough group. They are skeptical of me. I have tried being friendly, but they aren't having it. I get one-word answers to questions. Often, I'm completely ignored. If they don't want to do something, they simply don't do it. I know I must raise the standards. I am confident, though. If I teach them the correct way and explain the reason for the standard, they will get on board. *Right? They'll get on board.*

Yesterday, the issue was with green onions. "Hey, can you wash those green onions before you cut them?" I asked.

No answer. Deborah continued to cut the green onions.

I tried again. "Deborah, you have to wash those first. They're not clean and could make people sick." I had just finished my Food Safety Certification. I knew that unwashed produce creates the potential for food-borne illnesses like salmonella, listeria, or even hepatitis.

Deborah acted like she could not hear me. I physically went to her and said, "We can't use them if they aren't washed."

She walked away and muttered, "You do it, then."

I tossed the cut onions into the trash bin and grabbed a fresh bunch from the walk-in cooler. *How hard is it to wash the freakin' onions?*

I am not intimidated by Deborah, but her mother-in-law, who also works at the restaurant, I am careful with her. She's protective of her family. And, despite my fresh title of RGM, her mother-in-law clearly runs the restaurant. Her son also works at the restaurant, and he is intimidating. It's not due to the fact that he wears an ankle bracelet because he is just out of jail. It's his brooding that makes me nervous. He never looks at anyone. He never talks. He just shuffles around the restaurant like he's a slow-ticking time bomb.

The morning shift today is productive but quiet. The team goes about setting up the production line, cleaning the windows, and prepping for lunch. While I count the money in the safe, I keep one eye on Deborah. When she comes out of the walk-in with tomatoes and green onions to prep, I say "Deborah, please wash those."

She turns her head to glare at me and then reluctantly shuffles to the prep sink to wash the onions. *Round two: me.*

The rest of the morning is uneventful, but that ease ends at 12:15 pm. The dining room is jam-packed. My team is not well-trained or motivated, so service is slow, very slow. A man who's been waiting for a few minutes is tapping his drink cup on the front counter. *Tap, tap, …tap, tap, tap.*

The tapping rattles my nerves. I encourage the team to go faster. "Come on guys. Let's get these orders out."

They don't acknowledge me and seem to work even more slowly. I notice that Deborah has left her position on the line.

"Where's Deborah?" I ask.

Suddenly, she appears with a container of freshly-cut green onions. I hadn't noticed, but we had run out.

"Are those washed?" I ask. She stares at me. I grab the pan of onions from her and look at them while sorting through them with my hand. I can literally see the dirt. *Take a breath.*

I look her straight in the eye and say in a clear, loud voice, "If you can't follow my instructions and wash the onions, you can't work here."

All activity in the kitchen stops. No one moves. She slowly looks me up and down. Then she snarls, "Fine. We quit."

Deborah, Mama, and ankle-bracelet son walk out.

Before walking out the door, Mama Pack Leader yells across the dining room full of customers, "That bitch thinks she can run us outta here! She's gonna run you all out. Fuckin' bitch."

The entire restaurant comes to a standstill. The customers are silent. No one moves. I can feel fifty sets of eyes on her and then on me. My heart is pounding in my chest. I am genuinely afraid. *Deep breaths. Fight or flight? What should I do? This is not in the manual.*

The trio leaves the restaurant. I breathe a momentary sigh of relief, and then realize we have dozens of orders to make and no one to make them. I panic and start making tacos, burritos, Nachos Supremes, and Mexican Pizzas – without green onions – as fast as I can. Food is flying everywhere, and the orders keep coming.

I watch the clock on the Kitchen Display System monitor climb to fifteen and then twenty minutes. People are waiting twenty-five minutes for their lunch. They are demanding refunds. I can't even follow what is on the screen, so I'm just making whatever they say they ordered. I can hear someone in their car at the drive-thru window screaming at one of my few remaining team members, "I'VE BEEN SITTING IN THIS LINE FOR 25 MINUTES. WHAT THE HELL IS WRONG WITH THIS PLACE? WHO IS IN CHARGE? I WANT TO SPEAK TO THE MANAGER!"

I go to the window and profusely apologize. "Sir, I'm so sorry. No…no, you should never have to wait this long. I'm very sorry. Here's my business card. Please come by again and give us another chance."

I don't know how many customers simply walked out of my restaurant, never to return.

Mercifully, the rush ends around 1:30 pm. The dining room is a train-wreck. Every table is littered with trays and burrito wrappers. The beverage station is a sticky mess. The kitchen is even worse, with cheese, tomatoes, and lettuce all over the floor. We are supposed to do a "manager's walk" around the entire restaurant every thirty minutes. I haven't done the walk in over two hours. *Every thirty minutes. Yeah, right. Like I even have time to breathe.*

I wipe down the line and start to restock the ingredients. It's eerily quiet now. We are all a bit shell-shocked. No one is talking. Cheryl, my front counter cashier, grabs a spray bottle, towel, and a broom, and heads to the dining room. Christopher is sweeping the floor. I take a pan back to the dishwashing area and my jaw drops. Dirty dishes, trays, and pans are piled three feet high. It will take us hours to clean all this up. Christopher looks at me. "How about a cigarette?"

"Yes. That is a good idea."

We wander outside to the back of the restaurant for our three-minute break. The cold December air is refreshing. I can breathe. It is the first chance I have to even think about what happened. *What just happened?* I exhale and suddenly I'm exhausted. I am in shock, afraid and embarrassed. They just walked off. They were so angry, and they were angry at me. *What if they come back? How will I run this restaurant with three fewer people? What will I tell my boss? I'm sure he will see all the complaint calls. How did this happen?*

▪▪▪ Looking Back ▪▪▪

Being a restaurant general manager was the hardest job I ever had, way harder than being in the Army. It was so hard that I quit every day in my head, but I always came back the next day. I never cried in the Army, but I cried at Taco Bell. It seemed like the harder I tried, the worse I did. I mean – I did okay with customers, but I didn't understand how to manage labor and food costs. I often missed my monthly profit targets, therefore, I didn't get my bonus.

Then there were the team members. They were not "just like soldiers." Soldiers showed up for work. Soldiers wore their uniforms correctly. Soldiers knew how to do their jobs and didn't take short-cuts (most of the time). Soldiers obeyed orders, and, if they didn't, they got in big trouble, like going to jail. No, team members were not just like soldiers. They were a mystery. They would not show up for work or even call. They would come late and forget their name tag. Often, they couldn't or wouldn't follow procedures.

The most I could do was survive my shifts, pass the audits, try to hit numbers, go home, rest for a while, and then do it again the next day. In between lunch and dinner rush, I placed the food order, wrote the schedule, counted inventory, put the truck delivery away, organized the walk-in cooler, filed paperwork, and called in daily numbers.

In my thirty-year career, the day my team walked off was the worst day I had in a restaurant. I had plenty of train-wreck shifts in my career, but this was the worst. I can still hear the anger in the mother-in-law's voice as she says, "That bitch thinks she can run us outta here." My chest still tightens when I feel all those customers' eyes staring at me.

I have mentally replayed this experience hundreds of times. Why did it happen? Looking back with the perspective of experience, it happened because three team members got very angry and walked out. I never saw them again so I couldn't ask them, "Why were you so angry?" But, if I am being honest, I know exactly why they were angry. If I am being really honest, if I were in their shoes, I would have been angry too.

I strolled into that restaurant – large and in charge. I looked around and immediately began assessing everything: the sales, the profits, the people, the facility, the equipment, the service, the cleanliness. After my assessment, I decided what needed to be done, how it would be done, and how activities would be prioritized. I set goals. I made lists. I assigned tasks. I was focused and determined to get my restaurant headed in the right direction. After all, I was the restaurant manager.

Perhaps you are reading this story and can already see the problem. Everything started and ended with me. I was the superhero in my own movie. I would save the day. The problem was that I am only one person, and I could not do it alone, which became crystal clear when my staff walked out on me and fifty customers were staring at me.

Nonfiction authors (people who write books that are mostly true) often change the names of people who appear in their stories. I didn't have to change their names because I honestly cannot remember them. I never really learned their names. I didn't know where they were from or why they were working at Taco Bell. I didn't ask them what was important to them, or ask the names of their kids. I was so busy getting the work done that I hadn't bothered to get to know *them*.

Rather, I barged into their workspace with my newly-engraved name tag: Monica Rothgery, Manager, and began rearranging everything. I messed with their stations. I changed how things were organized and how things were done. I created disruption. I had good intentions, but it wasn't my restaurant. It was *their* restaurant, and I had no regard for them, the team, what they needed, and why they did things a certain way. They may have had very good reasons to put the hot sauce next to the drive-thru window instead of on the production line, like the manual says. They may have changed the corporate procedures to better serve their customers or to make a task easier. *I never asked them.*

Imagine what that must feel like. Your new boss marches into your office, sits down, and starts deleting files from your laptop and reorganizing your desk. Of course, they were angry. They had a right to be angry.

If I could do it all over, I would do it very differently. I would have set expectations with my boss. I would have told him that it was going to take a little time to get the restaurant on track. I would have taken the time to get to know my team. But the very first thing I should have done was to set expectations for myself. That turnaround was going to take time and I needed my team to be on board. There is an African proverb that says if you want to go fast, go alone but if you want to go far, go together. I needed my team.

Job one for the Superhero Manager is to let go of the superhero cape and win over the team. On my first day, I would have arrived with donuts. Every restaurant team loves donuts or ice cream or pizza. I would have methodically introduced myself and chatted with each of them, asking questions and listening to what was important to them. I would have scheduled fifteen-minute one-on-ones with every team member to sit down and hear about their family, their goals, and what makes them happy. The first meeting should have been focused on each of them as individuals, not the restaurant, its challenges, or my goals. I would have ended by asking one question: "What is one thing I can do to make you happier at work?"

> **Job one for the Superhero Manager is to let go of the superhero cape and win over the team.**

The answers to this question are often simple things.

"I need a name tag with my name spelled as Kathy, instead of Cathy."

"I'd like to get off at 3:30 instead of 4, so I can pick up my kids from school."

"Some days, I'd like to work the drive-thru window instead of making tacos."

"It would be great if the closing shift cleaned the floor drains."

The first step to building trust is doing the one thing that your team members ask for to make them happier at work. No one will care about the restaurant or the customers until you care about them first.

I had to keep showing that I cared. I had to honor their day-off requests. Ask about the score of their kid's soccer game. Post a calendar with their birthdays and work anniversaries so everyone knew they would be celebrated. They needed to know I cared. Only then could we start talking about goals for the team and the restaurant.

Next, I would have asked for and listened to their input on how we could make the restaurant better. Who do we want to be as a team? What do we want to be known for? Once a team commits to being the best at something, that is when the leader can lead. The goals are not Corporate's goals, or the manager's goals. They are the *team's* goals, and everything the team does is centered around achieving that goal – to be the fastest or the friendliest or have the most sales growth. The plan to accomplish the goal becomes the team's plan. The leader will train, coach, and guide.

That is when I could have introduced standards and processes.

"We can't be the best restaurant in Chicago if our restaurant doesn't sparkle."

"If we are going to be the fastest, everyone needs to show up for their shift on time. We need each other."

"We can't grow sales if customers get sick eating our food. So we have to wash the damn green onions."

I could have done a lot to avoid that nightmare shift. I could have learned their names and showed them I cared. I could have asked questions about their systems before I reorganized the restaurant and set lofty goals for them. I could have done all that and they still might have walked off because, in the end, people make their own choices.

Not every person will want to be on the team. Not everyone will commit to being a part of something bigger than themselves. Each person has a choice. They chose to move on. I had to move on. I had to find the next gem of a team member and start over building a team.

Lessons

- **First, show you care.** Nothing else matters until your team members believe that you will do anything for them. Once that happens, they will do anything for you.

- You have no goals. **There are only team goals.** The team sets the goals, and, with your leadership, they create the action plan.

- **Not everyone will want to be on the team.** It's not personal. Let them go – find your next all-star team member.

2

ROCKY AND BULLWINKLE

April 1993. Restaurant General Manager, Taco Bell, Westchester, Illinois

The months after the green onion incident are brutal as I try to find team members to work the day shift. Working short-staffed is no fun. The customers don't get good service, and the team feels the constant pressure. I am doing everything I can to recruit and hire new team members and, after several weeks, we have some new folks on board. They are slow and require a lot of attention, but at least we have people to help with the lunch rush.

I work the closing shift twice a week. It's not my favorite because we close at 1 in the morning, and I don't get home until 2:30 am. It makes for a really long night.

Tonight is one of those nights. I glance at my watch as I lock the drive-thru window. I can't believe it's already 1 am. It was a busy night for a Tuesday. I take the headset off and slip the battery into the charger. Frank is in the back doing dishes while Mo is mopping the lobby. I close the register and count down my drawer. I slip the cash into the safe drawer. With a heavy sigh, I pick up my clipboard and head into the walk-in cooler. *Weekly inventory counts SUCK!*

Everything in the restaurant needs to be counted and entered in the computer. The walk-in is freezing cold. I count as carefully and as fast as I can, knowing that if I miss a bag of lettuce, I will have to recount. I shiver as I scribble the numbers onto the inventory form, the lines too small to fit the numbers. I have learned to be very fast and very efficient. Seventeen minutes and I'm done.

Next is the task of converting boxes and bags of meat, chicken, and cheese to pounds. I took calculus in college, but, right now, I'm grateful for 9th grade math. Someday, someone will invent a computer program to do the calculation so all I will have to do is enter the number of boxes and bags, but today, I have to do math. I tabulate the inventory for all 120 items and enter the counts into the back-of-house computer. Now, to print it out. The slow printer begins its nightly slog – line by line – ever so slowly churning out the thirty pages of closing paperwork. I wait for the numbers that will tell me if it was a good week or another bad week.

I grab my ashtray that I hide in the bottom of the desk drawer and wander out to the dining room to light a cigarette. We aren't supposed to smoke in the restaurant, and, for safety reasons, we are forbidden to go outside after closing. So, what do I do? I smoke in the cold foyer, the space between the inner and outer door, blowing smoke through the cracks in the outer door.

I savor my three-minute smoke break and then they catch my eye: the two refrigerator-size boxes waiting for me in the corner. They have been taunting me all night. I dread opening them, but it needs to be done. I take one last drag from my cigarette and go search for the damn pink safety box cutter. The "safety knife" is carefully designed by some engineer at Corporate to prevent someone from cutting themselves. The problem is that it is also designed to prevent it from cutting ANYTHING. Most of my peers have a real razor blade hidden underneath the ashtray that they hide in the bottom desk drawer in the office, but the real razor blade is against policy. I'm too afraid to risk failing the safety audit.

The boxes are stamped with clear instructions – MANAGER: OPEN AND POST BY APRIL 7! That's tomorrow – we are starting a new promotion window. The boxes contain all the point-of-purchase material that I have to put up in my restaurant. It's like putting up Christmas decorations, but not nearly as fun.

I drag the boxes to the middle of the empty, clean dining room and fight with the pink non-cutter to get them open. It's 2 am and I'm tired. My shift started ten hours ago. I'm exhausted and my feet hurt. I force the box cutter into the cardboard and the handle snaps in two. *Damn it. Damn safety people. Damn Corporate who thinks this is a great idea: a box cutter that doesn't cut.*

Retrieving another cutter from my office, I notice that the printer has stopped its nightly slog. I take a deep breath. *Moment of truth.* I scan through the reports to get to the last line of the cost of sales report. I mutter to no one, "Please let it be good. Let it be good. Please God. Anything below 2.2%."

My eyes scroll, down, down, down to the last line. *Please let it be good.* It's 2.4%. *Not good.* I can feel the frustration crawling up from my stomach to my throat to my eye sockets. *No; I can't have another bad week. I'm going to get fired for sure. Why do I suck so hard at this?*

Back in the dining room, I manage to open the boxes and dump the contents on the floor. Shuffling through the assorted window clings, register toppers, and counter cards, I find the instructions. I take a moment to read about the free T-shirt promotion.

Buy 30 tacos, get a free Rocky and Bullwinkle T-shirt

RGMs (restaurant general managers, meaning me): Use the taco-shaped hole punch to punch the customer's card. One punch for every taco.

I find the hole punch, blink, and re-read the instructions:

One punch for every taco

I close my eyes and shake my head. My inner voice curses at the people in Marketing who have never worked the drive-thru window with seven cars in line. "Sorry you have to wait, Ms. Customer. The customer in the car ahead of you ordered ten tacos. I have to punch his Rocky and Bullwinkle card ten times."

We sell several hundred tacos a day. *Have they ever heard of carpal tunnel?* I set the punch and the cards by the register for tomorrow's training. Paula, my front counter cashier, is not going to like this promotion.

I put up the window clings and place the counter cards on the counter, but there are still two dozen pieces of random parts on the floor. Then I notice the instructions to the Rocky and Bullwinkle standee. I'm so tired my eyes can't focus and I'm cold, very cold. I never warmed up since I stood in the cooler. I read the instructions three times. Put tab A into part B. Slide C over B and flip into the base D. I slide A into B and C and D and step back. It falls over. I try again with the same result. Back to the instructions, which read like IKEA furniture assembly without the pictures. Again, it doesn't hold, and this step is just the first of six.

Come on, Monica. You are a smart, talented woman. You have a Bachelor of Science. You were a lieutenant in the United States Army. Surely you can put together a damn Rocky and Bullwinkle standee. Repeatedly, I read and try. Read and try. I think about the 2.4% on the report. Failure punches me in the gut. I sink to the floor and they come, gently at first and then without pause: the tears of fatigue and frustration. I can't do this.

I sit on the floor of my Taco Bell dining room as the tears fall. *I quit. I quit for real this time.* And if I don't quit, if I somehow survive and ever get out of here, I swear I will make it my life's work to make life easier for everyone who works in a restaurant. And if I ever meet the jerk who thought that a Rocky and Bullwinkle standee was a good idea, I'm going to punch him in the face.

Frank is waiting in the back for me. I call to him, "Let's get out of here."

Before I leave, I scribble a note to Daryl, my assistant manager.

Sorry about the mess in the dining room. I can't get the thing to stand. Maybe you can figure it out. Oh, and we blew food costs again. Watch the portioning, especially of cheese. Don't let them put too much on the tacos. See you around 11 am.

Despite quitting last night, I still get up in the morning and go to work. Once in the dining room, I am greeted by a six foot Rocky and Bullwinkle standee urging customers to buy 30 tacos to win a T-shirt. I wave to Paula. She holds up the taco-shaped hole punch, frowns, and shakes her head.

"I know… I know," I tell her. "Just do your best."

"What about speed?" she asks.

I shrug my shoulders. "Just do your best."

I know she is right. We will never make our speed numbers if we have to pause to punch the cards.

Daryl is the opening manager and has us ready for lunch rush. I ask him, "How did you get that Rocky and Bullwinkle thing to stand?"

"Easy!" he says casually. "I just followed the instructions."

■■■ Looking Back ■■■

The Rocky and Bullwinkle night pretty much shaped my entire career. I was sincere in my pledge to support restaurant managers because I didn't want anyone to struggle like I did. But I wonder – how much of that night was self-imposed suffering?

One of the first things I should have done was spend the money from my cash fund to buy a warm Taco Bell jacket or two from the uniform company. Sure, I would have had to watch my semi-variable spending for a few periods, but I deserved to be warm when I was in the cooler. And I only closed once or twice a week. My shift managers and my assistant manager closed the other nights. They were also shivering in the cooler, and THEY deserved to be warm.

It's a basic lesson. I learned it in the Army but had forgotten to apply it to my new job as a restaurant manager. It was my job to do everything I could to make it easy and comfortable for my team. I was being frugal with the company money, but it was short-sighted. My team deserved to have the uniforms, tools, and equipment to do their jobs. Yes, the pens, cleaning towels, and scissors were always disappearing, but that didn't mean they should be locked in the safe or the office. The team needed them.

The second thing I learned from Rocky and Bullwinkle was that I can't build stuff, so I shouldn't try. Why did I think I had to be the one to assemble the standee? Because the box said "Manager, post by April 7"? I struggled with that thing for over an hour in the middle of the night. It probably took Daryl ten minutes to put it together. Why did I think I had to do it?

There was nothing magical about putting up the promotional materials. It didn't require advanced leadership training or managerial skills. In fact, one of my team members would have enjoyed taking all the stuff out of the box and putting it up around the restaurant. A task I considered a chore could have been something new and interesting for them. How many other tasks was I doing that I could have delegated to another manager or a team member? That was when I learned that team members like to do new things.

So, I started experimenting. I taught Paula how to fill out the Daily Control Sheet when her shift was finished. She could count the money in her drawer and fill out the little form just as easily as I could. Sure, I had to check her deposit money to ensure it was all there, but I didn't need to count all the pennies, nickels, and dimes.

I taught Dennis how to prepare for the food delivery. The day before a truck delivery, Dennis would rotate the product on the shelf so the oldest ingredients were in front. He would clear out any empty boxes. He also started cleaning up the dry storage area because the shelves were mostly empty. Dennis oversaw the dry storage and the coolers. He liked the responsibility and the restaurant started to look more organized.

I had an assistant manager. He wanted to do more than run shifts, but I was holding onto everything because I thought I needed the control. I thought that I was the only one who could do it the "right way," but how was that working for me? I was over-tired and stressed out. My way was not working. So, we divided the work. I would do the schedule, and he would do the food order. I would do hiring, and he would take care of maintenance. We shared food safety and training.

That night was the start of my transition from manager who does it all to leader who engages her team. My team became more interested in our results, and our results got better. Sure, sometimes I had to work a position while one of my team members completed an administrative task like the Daily Food Safety Check, but it was worth the thirty minutes on the taco line to see them learn, grow, and take responsibility for our restaurant. Yes, "my" restaurant started to become "our" restaurant. The more they learned, the more they cared.

I did have to accept that no one did a task exactly the way I would do it. Sometimes they made mistakes, like forgetting a step in a process. Often, I had to keep coaching them on how to do something that I could do in my sleep.

Yes, it would have been easier to just do it all myself, but was that really serving me well? Or them?

In the beginning, I had to invest time into training and coaching my team, but, eventually, they got it, and then amazing things happened. They started to do tasks on their own. One afternoon, I was doing orientation for a new team member when I remembered that I hadn't done the daily safety check. Grabbing the clipboard with the checklist, I glanced down to see that Paula had already completed it. She beamed when I pointed to the clipboard and said, "Thanks. I really appreciate it."

I truly did. It was one less thing I had to do.

I learned one more thing that night about myself. I remembered that I had determination and perseverance. I remembered that I had grit: firmness of mind and spirit, courage in the face of hardship. The Army had taught me to push on, even when it was hard, even when I was cold and tired. This was no different. Sometimes it's hard. So what? Move on. Keep pushing. Keep doing the right thing. It will get better.

Once I accepted that sometimes running a restaurant is hard, I realized that I didn't have to suffer. *Okay, that happened. Now, what do I do about it? How do I solve it? What is the next step? Just keep going.*

Lessons

- **Take care of your team.** Provide them with everything they need to be safe, comfortable, and successful. It's your number one job.

- **Delegate.** Let your team members and junior managers help you. Let go of control and the need to do everything.

- **Develop your grit.** Some days are hard. Your hot line goes down, the sewer backs up, you miss your targets, you fail an audit – stuff happens. Clean up, restock, and move on.

3

WALK-IN COACH

April 1993. Restaurant General Manager, Taco Bell, Westchester, Illinois

It is a relief to have the Rocky and Bullwinkle promotion stuff posted. To my surprise, the team actually likes the T-shirts and goofy moose-antler hat that came in one of the big boxes. I make my way to the office to put my stuff down and poke my head out to ask Daryl, "Anything else going on?"

"No – oh, yeah, Phil called to say you-know-who is on her way here." He looks up from the drawer in which he's counting cash and can see the dread on my face.

"When did Phil call?"

"Oh, about an hour ago," he replies.

I take a deep breath. I'm half pissed off that Daryl didn't call to tell me that my boss is on her way to our restaurant. I'm also half grateful because there is less time to panic.

Phil manages the Taco Bell in the next suburb. There are about twenty of us in the area and we regularly call each other to try to keep one step ahead of our market coach. She's new to the company and she's never run a restaurant, as far as we know. She is tall and moves quickly. She is demanding and, well, quite intimidating. She's tough and not nice. In fact, she's mean. When they introduced her, I was excited to see a woman in the role, but now that I know her, I would rather have one of the experienced guys who knows how to run a restaurant.

"She's here!" Paula hollers and quickly puts on a headset so she can avoid any confrontation.

I see her beige Cadillac through the drive-thru window. Her tires squeal as she pulls into the parking lot. As she walks through the door, I can tell by her stride that she has reviewed the cost of sales numbers from last night. *This is not going to be good.*

My boss snarl-greets Cheryl, "Where's your name tag?"

"Right here," Cheryl replies as she fumbles to retrieve it from her pocket and pin it on her uniform.

"Good morning," I say meekly.

"Is it?" she asks as she plops her over-sized Louis Vuitton bag on my tiny office desk. "Have you seen the numbers?"

I nod my head as Daryl tries to scoot by me to hide in the back of the kitchen. The office is too small for this conversation, so she motions for us to head into the walk-in cooler.

Once in the cooler, she starts her rant. "Two point four? Two point four? Again? I thought we talked about this. The food cost target is two point two percent. Why is that so hard? This is the sixth time in ten weeks that you have missed the target. Phil can hit the target. Deb can hit the target. Yet, here you are again. Failing."

I swallow, shivering, and try to explain, "We have re-trained the entire team on portion control. We are tracking waste. We do extra inventory counts— We—"

She interrupts me. "Is it that you are incompetent, or you just don't care?"

I clench my jaw and glare. Her question hits like a direct punch to my heart. *I am giving my all to this damn job. Doesn't she understand?* It's a miracle that this place gets open every morning. Every day it is a different problem. Someone doesn't show up. The hot water tank goes out. The health inspector arrives during lunch rush. The food delivery arrives late or it's missing items that we need. Customers scream about incorrect orders. I'm perpetually exhausted and struggling. Every day is impossibly hard, and she heartlessly accuses me of not caring? *Fuck you.*

I can't hold back, and, for the second time in twelve hours, the tears come.

"Look, Monica. If you can't do it, I will find someone who can. It's that simple." She leaves the walk-in cooler and heads to the next restaurant on her list.

I stay in the cold for a few minutes longer, trying to regain some composure. Somehow, the cool air makes the pain less severe. I wipe my face on my shirt, take a deep breath, and go out to face my team and customers.

When I emerge, Daryl, Paula, and Cheryl have sympathetic eyes. They know what happened. The walk-in cooler is the woodshed, and I got my ass kicked again.

"I don't know how you do it. Makes me not want to get promoted," Daryl mumbles.

"It's okay. She's not wrong. Our food cost is too high, and it's my job to figure out how to fix it."

"Well, I don't know how it can be too high. We barely put any cheese on the tacos."

I don't know either, but I need to figure it out. That night, I lug all my reports home. I lay them out on my living room floor. I study ten weeks of numbers, trying desperately to find a trend, a reason that we are using more food than we are supposed to. I don't understand the connections.

I can't see what I'm missing, and I don't know what to do. In a final act of desperation, I call Phil. He has been doing this job for years and runs great numbers.

"Phil, hey, it's Monica. I need help." Saying those words feels like absolute defeat. I am the hotshot junior military officer they recruited. I have a fancy college degree, and here I am, needing help to save me from getting fired.

"Sure. I can help you. I'll come by tomorrow morning."

"You will? You can do that? You can leave your restaurant and come over to my restaurant?" I'm genuinely surprised. First, Phil has eagerly agreed to help me, and second, he can leave his restaurant during lunch. His restaurant is busier than mine.

True to his word, Phil shows up at my restaurant around 10 am. "Let's start by verifying your inventory."

"I just did the counts last night, but okay, if you say so."

After counting everything in the restaurant again, Phil and I sit in the dining room and review all my reports. He circles a few numbers and then suggests we go watch the team during lunch.

Phil shares his observations. "They are actually very good at portioning. Almost too good. They are not putting enough meat and cheese on the tacos. The customers aren't getting what they paid for, but I get why the team members are doing it. When you have food cost problems, the first place to look is portioning. You nag at them to not over-portion. So, they put less on the tacos."

After lunch, Phil shows me how to print some different reports – reports that I have never seen before. The one we are reviewing shows transactions, menu mix, and ticket averages. We sit in the dining room munching on burritos as he circles numbers. He points out that, on some shifts, there are very few drink orders, and that is a concern to him.

"Why would there be fewer drinks ordered, and why does that matter?" I ask. "Drinks aren't even in the calculation for food cost."

"See here," he points. "Some nights your ticket average is over six dollars but on other nights it is less than five. Hang on –"

Then, like a Jedi manager, Phil creates a little chart and scribbles in numbers. Pouring through the reports strewn across three tables and aided by a pocket calculator, Phil does his magic. Finally, he leans back in his chair and clasps his hands behind his head. Quite pleased with himself, he announces, "I know your problem."

"What? What is it?" I ask pleadingly.

"You have a thief. Someone on your team is stealing from you."

▪▪▪ Looking Back ▪▪▪

A few lessons were learned from this experience. One was, and it may be stating the obvious, but unless there is imminent danger, no one should be yelled at in their place of work. My experience with the market coach in the walk-in cooler was not okay. She belittled and threatened me. She accused me of not trying when I was trying my heart out. Short of quitting, what could I have done differently? Maybe nothing. She had the power and was abusing it.

I could have reported her to Human Resources, but that never occurred to me. I could have left the company. I chose to stay because I was too tired to find another job. I did have one more choice, a choice that I didn't know about until years later. If I had known, I could have chosen to ignore her. I could have brushed off her attack like a pesky fly at a picnic. I could have stepped into my truth.

Although I was struggling, I knew I was a good leader and what she said didn't matter. She was not speaking the truth about me. I was not incompetent, lazy, uncaring, or stupid. I did not have to invest my self-worth in her approval. Who cared what she thought of me? Yes, I needed to hit my targets, but I didn't need to internalize her labeling of me – which was not an easy thing for me to do, because I wanted her to believe in me, to respect me. But she wielded approval like a weapon. Instead of standing there and taking it, I could have learned to duck and avoid absorbing this attack in my heart and my mind. I couldn't dismiss her completely, and I certainly couldn't yell back at her. But I didn't have to let her perspective annihilate my self-worth.

After a few months, she left the company. She was gone. No more yelling or abuse. They said she moved on to "a new opportunity." The truth was she was not a fit for the company. And to think, I almost let her, someone I would never see again, undermine my self-worth. *Screw you, mean lady! I am a good leader and a dedicated employee, even if I haven't figured out food cost yet.*

The thing about bad bosses is they can also be role models who showcase what NOT to do. That boss showed me the kind of leader I would never want to be. I decided that I would never be a leader who screamed or demeaned. I didn't want to be a leader who used fear as a weapon to get better performance. I knew that, but until I experienced what it was like to be treated poorly, I didn't really understand how much damage a leader can do. I know I was not always perfect, but I made it my goal to lift my team up, cheer them on, and let them know I believed in them. If they screwed up, we would have a conversation about how to improve, but it was never a personal attack. I strove to be the kind of leader who I wanted to follow myself.

Another thing I learned from this experience was to swallow my pride and ask for help. I was a new manager, and there was a lot I didn't know. I didn't know what I didn't know. I knew that theft was a possibility, but I never really thought that one of my team members would steal. Not knowing something is not my fault. No one can be expected to perform well if they are not taught how to do a task. However, not asking for help? That was one hundred percent on me.

I now realize that I was not alone. I could have called Phil much earlier, but I was too proud, too worried that

I would be exposed. I was embarrassed that they would discover the hotshot college grad army officer couldn't do the job.

The reality was that Phil was happy to help me. Sure, he teased me a bit, but it wasn't cruel, and it didn't hurt me anywhere near as bad as being called a failure by my boss. I was new, and he had years of experience.

Another interesting thing happened when I asked for help: I became one of the gang. I was no longer the outsider, the "external hire." I was just another manager trying to get by. Being honest about my problems created a newfound trust and more honesty. A few years later, when I had more experience, some of my peers would ask me for help. I remember that a few of the more seasoned managers would come by after the end of the quarter. They would bring their financial reports and ask me to calculate their bonuses, since the formula was a bit complicated, and I was good at math. I didn't gloat or judge them. I was genuinely happy to help them and appreciated that they trusted me. That only happened because I reached out first. My peers weren't the competition. They were allies and resources.

Lessons

- **It takes courage and confidence to resist a boss who is a bully.** Believe in yourself. If you need some moral support, reach out to those who love and care for you: family, friends, peers, and mentors.

- **Be better than your boss.** Use experiences with negative bosses to become the kind of leader you want to follow. Challenge yourself never to use cheap tactics like belittling someone to get results.

- **Ask for help.** You are not alone. No problem is new. Someone has already found a solution. Be vulnerable and admit you need help.

4

QUEEN OF THE DRIVE-THRU

May, 1993. Restaurant General Manager, Taco Bell, Westchester, Illinois

Phil leaves me a list of things I can do to try to discover who is stealing from our store. I am skeptical because I can't believe someone on my team would steal. Reluctantly, I take Phil's advice and start checking the dumpster at odd hours. I am looking for bags of chicken or nacho chips that someone took out with the trash to pick up later. I drive by my restaurant on my day off to look for anything unusual. I find nothing, but the numbers seem to get better. We make our targets for a few weeks in a row, and some of the pressure eases.

It's late afternoon on a Wednesday, and all my high school kids are coming in for their shifts. I love this time of the afternoon and the energy they bring. They cruise in, chatting about school and complaining about teachers and homework. As they check the deployment chart to see what position they are working, they tease each other about who is slowest on the line. Janice clocks in and so does Sara, the mom of the group. She has five kids and works from 4 to 8 pm, Monday through Thursday. I count the cash for Sara's drawer and send her off to the drive-thru window, where she is the self-proclaimed "Queen of the Drive-Thru."

Honestly, she deserves the title. She is always ten minutes early and is ready to go at 4 pm sharp. The customers LOVE her. They greet her by name at the drive-thru speaker: "Hey, Sara. I'll take my usual."

She recognizes the voice and punches six Soft Shell Taco Supremes and a large Pepsi into the point-of-sale system. She knows exactly how to time her work, so she is ready to greet her customer at the window with a heartfelt, "What's up? How've you been? How's your little one?"

She also knows the exact price of every menu item, so she is super fast. This goes on all evening long. When she doesn't have a customer, she jokes around with the kids on the line. I love her. She has the best attitude and is a dream employee.

It gets busy around 6 pm, so I throw on a headset to help where I can. Push A on the headset, and we can talk to the customer at the drive-thru menu board.. Push B, and we can talk to each other. The banter is fast and funny.

Chris says, "Alert – boss on the headset. Watch the language!"

I press B and say, "Your vocabulary is broad. Why would you default to F-bombs?"

Chris replies, "Because it's fucking funny," and they all crack up like the high school kids that they are.

I roll my eyes at them as I bag a couple of Burrito Supremes and head to the drive-thru window to hand the food to a guy in a Ford F-150. "Do you need any sauce?"

"Nah, I'm good," he says. "I just need my drink."

"Your drink?" I ask because I hadn't noticed a beverage on his order.

"Yeah, large Pepsi. It's right there."

Sure enough, a large drink is sitting on the window, which I hand to him along with a straw while muttering, "Have a nice evening."

I go back to check his order on the POS (point of sale) screen – I really don't remember seeing a drink included in that order. His order is already bumped off as completed. I move on to the next order and don't think any more about it until, a few cars later, it happens again. The customer at the window has paid for her order and is waiting for her food. I finish bagging her food, toss the receipt in the bag, and then I notice that she is sipping a large soda. I quickly pull the receipt out of the bag and read it:

1 Mexican Pizza
2 Tacos

There is no drink on her order and yet, there she is, drinking a large soda. The pit in my stomach forms slowly. *Why are people getting drinks but they are not on the receipt or on the screen? OMG. No...no...no... not my Sara. She can't be the one. NO! Not her.*

Now, I am watching very carefully, and the sinking feeling grows. Whenever a customer orders a large drink, Sara doesn't ring it up on the system, but she sells the drink to the customer. He pays for what he gets, except Taco

Bell isn't getting the money for his drink. A large drink is $1.06, so Sara can easily add the amount to the order and charge the customer the correct amount. The happy customer pulls away and Sara's drawer is over $1.06.

I literally want to throw up. I am sick with betrayal and angry, so angry. I know what I need to do. Without warning, I pull her register drawer in the middle of her shift and give her a new drawer. Sara sees what I'm doing and starts to freak out, screaming at me, "What are you doing? That's my drawer! You can't do that. I'm not done working."

I glare at her as I snatch the printout off the POS printer and close my office door. I begin to count. That printout will tell me everything. Ten minutes later, my suspicion is confirmed. The drawer is over $6.36. Six large drinks were not entered into the system. Not only that, but Phil taught me to look for a tracking system, and I find it. Every time she pulled her con, Sara put a penny in the spare coin slot. When she got to ten pennies, she would slide a ten-dollar bill out of the drawer and into her pocket. She had an even more elaborate scheme to track the change. Over the course of her four-hour shift, she was likely stealing $25 in cash every night. It doesn't sound like a lot, but she was doubling her income tax-free, and we were losing four hundred dollars in sales every month, enough for us to miss our sales targets and impact the food cost percentage.

When I open the door, Sara screams that I had no right to pull her drawer, and she is not doing anything wrong. She pushes her way past me, grabs her purse, and screams at me as she heads for the door. "You fucking bitch!"

I never see her again.

I am heartbroken. The rest of the shift is somber. I ask Janice, my closing shift manager, if she minds if I leave early, and, for the first time ever, I leave before my shift is over. I go home, crack open a beer, and stare at the TV, lost in self-pity, rage, and intense disappointment. All this time, I had been getting screamed at, threatened, and made to feel like I was a loser by my boss, being told that I was the worst manager. All this time, it was Sara, my most trusted team member. *What will I tell her customers? How did I miss this?*

■■■ Looking Back ■■■

Sara was my thief. She was my most treasured employee, a customer favorite, reliable, fun – and a thief. Her con was quite impressive. She had me so focused on her service and positive energy that it never even occurred to me that she could be taking money from the register. It was a perfectly executed act.

I felt disoriented and deceived, and I was down a team member again. But an amazing thing happened. After I fired Sara, I consistently hit my food cost targets every week for months on end. It was a relief to have the problem solved and I learned a lot.

I learned that, while I want to always trust my team members, anyone is capable of anything. Trust, but verify. In today's environment, most restaurants have reports that flag suspicious activity like inconsistencies in ticket average or cars per hour through the drive-thru window. These reports help managers identify potential areas of concern. Yet many managers don't look at these reports. Maybe, like me, they don't want to believe someone on their team is stealing, or maybe they are afraid to discover that their best shift manager is helping themselves to extra cash.

I learned not to be blind-sided the way I was with Sara. Instead, I learned to stay neutral when it came to my team members. I loved them. I cared for them, and knew any one of them was capable of making poor choices. If they chose a bad path, I had to do my job. They couldn't be on my team.

I wince when I hear managers describe their team members like family. My team was not my family. They were my team. I love my family members no matter what. I would never fire my family. My loyalty to my team, however, was not unconditional. I expected certain principles and behaviors. If someone could not follow the team rules, they could not be on the team. The team expected me to act. They didn't like it when the rules weren't enforced.

> If someone could not follow the team rules, they could not be on the team.

I learned to never be surprised by what some people will do. It felt personal, but it wasn't. I have no doubt that, a week after getting fired from my restaurant, Sara was at another fast-food restaurant, memorizing the menu and prices while she wowed her customers and managers with great service.

Lessons

- **Trust, but verify.** Love your team, and remember that anyone, even your best employee, can make a poor choice. If they make a poor decision, it is your job to hold them accountable. Your job is to protect the team and the business.

- **Your team is not your family.** Your team expects you to uphold the standards and hold others accountable. Sometimes that means you must let people go. It's never easy, but it's your job.

- **Every problem has a solution.** Keep searching for data and resources. Stay open to all possibilities. Ask everyone. The resolution might be right in front of you.

5

WE'RE OUT OF BEANS

September 1993. Restaurant General Manager, Taco Bell, Westchester, Illinois

"Welcome to Taco Bell #4442. My name is Monica, and I am the Restaurant General Manager. I'm in charge of everything that happens here. I hire and train new people. I make sure we serve great-tasting food and have friendly service. I'm in charge of safety, equipment maintenance, and cleanliness. I forecast sales, order the food, and manage inventory. I write the schedule. I manage labor costs, food costs, and cash to make sure we make a profit. I make sure money gets to the bank."

I started doing tours for students as part of community outreach and to showcase our Taco Bell restaurants. I show the kids the heavy, metal safe that is bolted to the floor in the kitchen. The little kids are the best. They marvel at the awesomeness of the sour cream gun and ask the best questions, like, "How do you know a car is outside if you can't see it from inside?"

"Who wants to work the drive-thru window?" I ask.

Six hands shoot up. I pick one of the middle-schoolers and slip a headset over his hairnet. They have to wear hairnets in the kitchen, which makes them all giggle.

"I look like my grandma," one little girl declares.

"The two most important things we do is to serve our customers safe, delicious food, and to serve them very fast. The idea of fast food is that it's fast, right?" The kids nod in agreement. They take turns trying on the drive-thru headset and listening to customers and, finally, head out to the dining room to munch on their free taco and drink their small Pepsi.

I say goodbye to the kids and go check on whether we are ready for the lunch rush. "Rush ready" is a process, and every process in a restaurant has a checklist. I pull *my* checklist from the office and give it a run-through. Yes, it is *my* checklist. I've been leading this restaurant for about nine months now. I no longer just use what Corporate gives us. While the corporate checklist is a good starting point, they forget speed – and important tasks such as charging the headset batteries and checking for a full roll of paper in the register printer. Taking time out during lunch to refill printer paper kills speed.

Armed with my list, I do my manager's walk. I start on the line. Hot food is prepped with backups in the heated cabinet. Cold food is on the line. Packaging is stocked. There is change in the register drawers. Soda boxes are full. The drive-thru window sparkles. *I hate a dirty drive-thru window.* Checking the dining room, the ice bin is full, and napkin holders are stocked. Toilet paper is in the restroom. A quick walk outside, and I see a clean parking lot. I can't find one cigarette butt. *Mental note – Tell Dennis he did a great job on the lot.* Heading to the back, I see Dennis finishing up the dishes and Cheryl completing the Daily Food Safety Checklist. We are rush ready!

"Nice job on the lot, Dennis!" I holler so he can hear me over the sound of the dishwasher.

The best part is that the team is all here. No one called off. With my dry-erase marker in hand, I fill in the deployment chart, a layout that shows each team member their assignment for the lunch rush. "Aces in their places" is what the training manual says.

Super-friendly Paula is always on front cashier. The regulars love her, and she takes care of the dining room. Dennis doesn't read the order screen too well, so he's on food prep and dishes in the back. I put Pam and Cheryl on the food line. No team is faster at making tacos and burritos. The last position to assign is the drive-thru window, the most important position – the epicenter of our lunch rush and key to hitting our speed goals for the entire day. Who do I put there? Who is the best at multitasking? Who can do both friendly and fast with mind-blowing efficiency? *Me!* I write "Monica" in the drive-thru position. No one can run drive-thru like I can.

"Okay, guys, let's make it a great lunch," I holler to my team as I put on the drive-thru headset.

DING! The headset goes off. A car is at the menu board.

"Welcome to Taco Bell. Would you like to try our new Seven Layer Burrito?" I ask quickly. The suggestive selling is annoying because the customer probably already knows what they want to order, but it's required. I'll lose points on a customer audit, so I don't skip it.

"Nope. Give me two Burrito Supremes and a small Pepsi."

"That will be $2.72. Please pull around." As he pulls up to the window, I pour the drink. Once he is at the window, I take his cash and hand him his drink. "You need any sauce?"

"Hot," he mutters.

DING!

"Welcome to Taco Bell. Would you like to try a Seven Layer Burrito ?" I hand the first guy his food and he drives off.

"Um, no. I'll have a Mexican pizza with sour cream and a medium Pepsi."

"That's $2.41. Please pull around." I pour the Pepsi and take his payment.

"Here you go. Have a nice day." I hand him his food and drink and move to take the next order.

Working drive-thru is the apex of multitasking. It's a game. When a car pulls up to the window, it triggers a sensor. The sensor is connected to a timer inside the restaurant. The timer hangs right above the drive-thru window and counts the seconds a car is sitting. The game is to get the car to pull away from the drive-thru window as fast as possible. That is why some places (not ours) post a sign admonishing their customers: "Have your money ready when you get to the window." They want you to pull away fast.

Speed targets are a big deal, and managers look for every advantage. I've heard stories that some managers will drive circles around their restaurants, pausing for a few seconds at the window. This strategy lowers their overall average, but cheating never works. Driving around and around creates a red flag on the Exception Report. The system notices if there are lots of cars with no sales. Instead of cheating, we work on being as fast as possible.

Car after car cruises through. We are averaging forty seconds per car. I'm in a groove until I hear Cheryl holler from the food line, "Monica, we are out of beans."

"Use your backups," I holler back to her.

"I'm on my last pan."

"Okay. Ask Dennis to make three more pans," I say before getting back to the drive-thru.

DING!

"Welcome to Taco Bell. Would you like to try a Seven Layer Burrito?"

I enter a Nachos BellGrande and a large Mountain Dew into the point of sale and tell the driver to pull around. From the back of the kitchen Dennis appears. "Monica, we are out of beans."

I admonish Dennis. "I know. I asked Cheryl to tell you to make three more pans. Come on now. You know what to do."

Dennis scampers off and I take the next order, pour the drink, and hand out food at the window. A few minutes later, I feel a *tap, tap, tap* on my arm.

DING!

I look over; it's Dennis.

"Welcome to Taco Bell. Please hold." In an impatient tone, I say, "DENNIS! WHAT?"

He hesitates, so I look at him – really stop to look. My dear team member is dripping with sweat. His eyes are as wide as saucers. I see panic and dread in them. He wipes the sweat from his brow and says in a slow, measured voice, "Monica, we are out of beans."

Everything stops at that moment. *My God, no! That's impossible.*

I race back to the dry storage area. Where there should be boxes and boxes of refried beans, there is nothing but air. We are not just out of prepared beans. We are out of beans. The entire restaurant is out of beans. No beans. None.

Through my headset, I hear, "HEY, HEY – is anyone there? How long do I have to wait?"

"Sorry about the wait, sir. Go ahead with your order."

"Yeah, I'll have two Bean Burritos."

No, no you won't. I swallow to try to find my voice. "Um, I'm sorry, sir. We are temporarily out of beans. Would you like two Beef –"

The customer erupts. "WHAT? ARE YOU KIDDING ME? HOW THE FUCK ARE THERE NO BEANS AT TACO BELL?"

The millstone of shame and blame sits squarely on my shoulders. I send Dennis to borrow beans from a nearby restaurant, and, for the next two hours, I watch my team members explain to customer after customer that we, Taco Bell #4442, are out of beans.

Alone in my tiny office, I process my mistake. I had failed to do my job. It is my job to make sure we have enough ingredients. It is my job to make sure the inventory is correct. I let my customers down. I let my team down. *Why did I fail to do my job? How did this happen?*

■■■ Looking Back ■■■

On that fateful day, we ran out of beans because I didn't do my job. My job was to make sure we had enough beans for the shift. I was so busy being the "Champion of Speed" that I failed to do what was mine to do. If I do not do what is mine to do, no one else will. I could work a team member position like the drive-thru position, but no one could work my position – doing what is mine to do. Of all the lessons I learned from working in a restaurant, this one was the most important.

> **If I do not do what is mine to do, no one else will.**

The "Day Without Beans" was the last day I put myself in a team member position. Instead, I learned to lead the restaurant team. The first thing I learned was to observe. I never realized how little I watched my team work together. I was amazed at the little things I saw. There were so many things I could do to help make their jobs easier. One improvement was to move the burrito wraps closer to the ground beef. It saved the team members a few seconds. I saw that the nacho cheese pump got clogged during lunch and slowed down the line. So, I ordered a backup pump. I adjusted the monitor height so they didn't have to arch their necks to see the screen. I put up job aids to remind them to put sauce and napkins in the bag.

I realized that, during some shifts, the team did not understand how to stay in position. They were wasting time running around each other. So, we focused on communication. I put tape on the floor and made a game of telling them they could not move off the tape. Instead, they had to talk to each other and ask for what they needed. I learned how to coach. I discovered the power of observing and listening to my team perform during peak periods. I could cheer them on, celebrate their wins, and point out little and big ways to improve. I realized I couldn't lead them if I was locked in a position.

I also started going into the dining room and talking to my customers. I began to build relationships with them. I got to know them. They weren't just transactions. They were people. One Italian couple would come in every Sunday after church. I looked forward to their weekly visit. They even invited me over to dinner (I think they wanted me to meet their son). I still have the pesto recipe they gave me. I would not know them if I had been locked in at the drive-thru position – or any position.

Interesting things happened when I started focusing on doing what was mine to do – the team got better, more efficient, and more independent. We got faster, and I had more time to do other tasks. I had time to do more community outreach, which helped grow sales. I had time to teach my shift managers how to become coaches. I had time to think about service and how to improve. By developing my team, I created an environment where I wasn't needed in a position and could focus on running the business like a general manager.

I realize this is a controversial topic. Many people in the industry will say that the manager needs to be on the line or in a position – for two reasons. First, the cost of labor. Second, there is a belief that a manager who works a position shows the team that they are right there with them. They believe it is an example of servant leadership. These are myths.

The first myth is that the cost of labor forces managers to work the line. In some low-volume restaurants, this may be true. If the restaurant is so slow that only three people are working, the manager will need to help serve guests. However, in most restaurants, a manager working the line is not a good use of labor. It is a waste of labor. The manager working in a team member position is a very expensive team member. Meanwhile, they aren't running the restaurant, training their team, growing the business, or finding ways to improve profitability.

The second myth is that working in a position shows the team that you care. The truth is that team members in a properly staffed restaurant do not need or want the manager to work in a position. They don't want them sitting in the office or talking on the phone for hours, either. What they want is for the manager to do their job. Team members want to work with other trained team members. They want equipment that works and the restaurant to be organized. They want to work in a clean environment. They want the manager to do something about the

Servant leadership is not doing the team member's job. Servant leadership is doing everything you can to support them, coach them, and celebrate them.

guy who is always late. They want the manager to make sure the night shift stops leaving a pile of trash by the back door. Servant leadership is not doing the team member's job. Servant leadership is doing everything you can to support them, coach them, and celebrate them.

As Chief Operations Officer at KFC, it was not uncommon for me to be in a restaurant talking to the restaurant manager as he nervously watched the order monitor, anxious if three orders popped up.

"Excuse me, Monica. I have to get the orders out." He would hurry over to the line, sometimes pushing team members out of the way to make the food and clear the screen. I would shake my head as the team members drifted off to get a drink while the manager did their job.

I'm not saying that managers should never help. Sometimes, there is an unexpected surge in orders, or the team gets in the weeds. Of course, the manager should offer to help – and that is the key. Ask your team, "Do you want me to jump in?"

Most times, they will say "no" and work through it. If they say "no," then don't jump in. Instead, ask, "How can I help?" Maybe they need some ingredients brought out from the back or for the line to be wiped down. They will tell you if you ask them. They will learn to work their way out of the weeds. By asking how you can help, you show them respect. You show that you're there if they need you, but you don't rescue them. You build pride and trust.

The best example I ever saw of this trust and support was at the KFC in Yuba City, California. As COO, I traveled all over the United States, visiting restaurants. In 2022, I made the trek to Yuba City to visit the busiest KFC in the country. Yuba City had a population of less than 100,000, yet they had the highest volume KFC. How did they do it? I had to know their secret.

It looked like a normal KFC from the outside. It was a single-lane drive-thru, and, interestingly, the franchisee, Justin Stewart, had designed an outdoor order-taking position. His team created their own mobile order-entry system on a tablet and somehow integrated it into the KFC system. He had built a covered area with fans to keep his team members cool. Even though none of this detail was in the KFC operating system, Justin was doing what he could to support his team and grow sales. He had learned how to do what was his to do!

Inside the restaurant, however, I was disappointed. While it was spotless and organized, with the team efficiently going about their work and customers coming and going, there was no magic, no secret recipe. It was all normal KFC stuff. I assumed it was a slow day. I couldn't wait to meet the RGM.

Justin beamed. "This is Sergio. He is the manager of the busiest KFC in the United States."

"It is so incredible to meet you. Your restaurant is beautiful. Amazing, truly amazing, what you have done here. If you have time, can you show me around your restaurant? I want to meet your team."

Sergio was relaxed and smiled. "Of course, I have time. My team has everything covered." We headed to the kitchen to start the tour.

I looked at the order screen. It had a few orders, though hardly what I would expect for the busiest restaurant in the country. "It seems really slow. Is the heat wave keeping people away?"

Sergio looked at me, surprised. "Slow? No, it's not slow. In fact, we are having a super busy day. We are on track to have the busiest day of the month."

I looked around in disbelief. "How is that possible? It's so calm."

"Easy," he said. "Everyone is doing their job. They know what to do, and they do it. I never work the line. I just walk around and make sure everyone is okay and having a good time. Sometimes, I get something they need from the back. Mostly, though, I talk to the customers and coach my team."

Sergio knew the lesson. He was doing what was his to do. Recently, Sergio was promoted to Area Coach. Now, he helps other restaurant managers learn how to lead their restaurants and discover what is theirs to do.

Throughout my career, I practiced this lesson daily. I asked myself, "What is mine to do? Is this project, presentation, or research mine to do? Or is this a chance to teach, empower, or coach someone on my team?"

This lesson was not about dumping work on my people or never chipping in to help them out. Instead, it was about challenging myself to understand *what was mine to do*. The question helped me think bigger and be more strategic. It took me out of the weeds and helped me be proactive and strategic. The team grew. I grew, and the business grew.

Lessons

- **Do what is yours to do.** There is no one else who can do what you need to do. Let your team do their job. If you're not sure what is yours to do, talk to your coach or ask successful leaders in your organization.

- **Develop your team.** Teach them to do what you can do so they become self-sufficient instead of overly dependent.

- **Admit when you made a mistake.** Fix it. Learn from it, and move on.

6

HOW HARD IS IT TO CLEAN?

*December 1993. Team Unit Manager, Taco Bell,
two restaurants in the Chicago suburbs*

After managing Westchester for one year, I am promoted to Team Unit Manager and assigned a second restaurant in Berwyn, Illinois. *Can't even handle one, and now they want me to do two?* It's my first day, and I am greeted by a chorus of "hellos." I make my way through the kitchen with two dozen donuts. I take my time, meeting each team member. I know now how important this first impression is. *I am not going to screw this up again.* I exhale a sigh of relief. *This group is much friendlier than my first team.*

As I look around to see who is in charge, the office door opens and a man growls, "I'll be out in a minute."

The team members smile uncomfortably. "That's Craig, the assistant manager," says Melissa, who is working the drive-thru window.

I smile. *Warm and fuzzy is over.*

Twenty minutes later, Craig emerges and offers to show me "his store." As Craig shows me around, he makes it very clear that he is the one who "keeps the store running on track." He informs me that his schedule is set in stone. He works Wednesday to Friday, and Sunday, and closes Tuesday night, because it's end-of-week counts, and he is the only one who can count correctly.

As we walk around the restaurant, I am shocked at the lack of cleanliness and organization. The back area is a mess, with old, unused equipment stacked up. As we make our way to the office, I note build-up on the baseboards, the cracked ceiling tiles, and a leaky sink. At the door to the office, I gasp. The desk space is covered with papers, mail, and burrito wrappers. Outdated marketing material is piled up on the tiny office shelves. The lieutenant in me bristles. *OMG! This is FUBAR!* (that's Army-speak for "f***** up beyond all recognition")

Craig shuffles some papers aside and then points to the spot where he hides his ashtray. I smile at him knowingly and say, "THAT is good to know." All the while, my eyes are absorbing this cyclone of an office.

Craig grabs various papers from multiple stacks, and we head to the dining room. As we review the numbers, Craig is clearly proud that he consistently hits his labor and food cost targets. Customer service scores are good, too. So is speed! Not surprisingly, they are also hitting the sales targets because they have good service and speed.

I wait for him to get to food safety. He goes on talking about the team members, shift managers, who works what positions, and the schedule (which he does on Sundays). Still, he doesn't talk about the food safety score. He clearly needs me to acknowledge him as the leader and not mess with his restaurant. At the same time, I was sent here for a reason, and it is not because everything is "on track."

"Hey Craig, it's such a relief that you have a good handle on food and labor. I'm also excited we are hitting sales. My other restaurant struggles to hit the sales targets. How about food safety?"

He rolls his eyes as if he knew this question was coming. "Yeah, well, our auditor is a dick, so we have failed two times in a row."

"Hmm, that sucks," I say, trying to show some half-hearted empathy. "Could I see the reports from the auditor?"

"They are around here somewhere," he mumbles as he shoves stacks of paper on top of other stacks of paper and then says, "Hey, we need to get out there for lunch peak."

Working the lunch shift is fun. The team is playful. They know the customers, who seem to appreciate the relaxed atmosphere. I can't help but wonder how no one else sees the dirt. There is a thick layer of dust on top of the stainless steel cabinets. Cobwebs dangle off the wires and cords that hang from broken ceiling tiles. The team members' uniforms are stained and worn. The more I look, the more problems I see, the biggest of which is going to be convincing Craig that we have a problem. We will never pass the food safety audit if we don't get the place clean.

After the lunch rush, I go into the office and print the reports from the last two audits, doubtful that I will find the originals. I order a chicken burrito for myself and invite Craig to join me in the dining room. I study the reports. They got two "F" ratings in the last two quarters. Fail your audit, and you lose that quarter's bonus. Fail three times and the manager gets fired. It is a very difficult inspection, easy to fail – an unforgiving policy.

Craig sits down next to me. I begin. "The good news is that the team members are well-trained. No points were deducted for team member mistakes. They know what to do, which means you have trained them well." I try to sound reassuring because the reality is his ass is on the line. He knows it. "So, the deductions are all for cleanliness, maintenance, and organization. If we work together with the team, we can clean this place up, and we will have no trouble passing the next one."

I watch Craig slowly look around the dining room: at the dirty windows, black grout, and stained ceiling tiles. He looks resentful and defeated. The restaurant hasn't had a general manager for six months, and Craig is alone.

Attempting to reassure him, I say, "You have had to do this all by yourself, and it's hard, really hard. But now, you're not alone. I can help."

He looks at me skeptically and sighs. "Okay," he says quietly.

So begins the work of a massive deep clean plan.

The hard part is we don't have any extra labor hours to dedicate to the deep clean. Instead, we have to squeeze extra cleaning into the regular schedule. I work with each shift to create a detailed plan. Each team member is assigned a cleaning challenge: an area to clean and keep clean. I put up a big sign next to the schedule.

> **Pizza Party!**
>
> **Once everyone completes their cleaning challenge.**
>
> **WE can do it!!!**

Surprisingly, the promise of a pizza party creates some positive buzz, and the team gets into it. Every day, we look a little cleaner. I delegate what I can, and yet still find myself scrubbing baseboards. I purge the tiny office, tossing out years of old paperwork. I am on the phone for hours with vendors trying to get new ceiling tiles and fix leaky faucets and floor cracks. It's been a month, and we are starting to look pretty good. I put up notes regularly to encourage the team.

> **Great Job Team!**
>
> **It's looking great around here. Now we have to keep it clean.**
>
> **Let's make sure we have good closing shifts!!**

The truth is that everyone prefers to work in a clean and organized environment. It is just easier. I am confident we will pass the next audit, Craig will stay employed, and we will have our pizza party, EXCEPT for one unexpected variable– Melissa.

Melissa is one of my closing shift managers. She is so sweet and tries so hard. She is a newer shift manager, so I never know exactly how she will leave the restaurant at closing. When I arrive in the morning, I find the note she left.

> *Hi Monica. Busy night. Great close, though. Frankie went home early because he didn't feel good. I had to help Chris, so I couldn't finish inventory. Sorry…*

I sigh, resigned to the fact that I have to scramble to finish her work and complete the morning manager tasks. I look around the kitchen – it's a mess. There's trash in the bins. The cold well has shreds of cheese in it, and the warming cabinets are full of crumbs. The stainless steel cabinet handles are caked with daily grime, and the soda machine wasn't even disassembled for cleaning. The dining room tables look clean from a distance, but when I look closer, I find sticky soda rings on nearly half of the tables. *Mental note – Coach Melissa on cleanliness.*

I make a list of all the issues and leave a note in the manager's log.

> *Melissa, thanks for the note. Sorry that you had to work extra to help Chris. Hey, I need you to work more on cleaning because there was a lot of stuff to clean in the morning. Check the list before you leave!*

Yet, every morning, I find the same issues. I leave more lists and more notes. I even call during her shift to remind her, but Melissa's closing shifts are always a mess. My mornings are now a rat race as we clean up after Melissa's shift. I am constantly worried about failing the audit. *How hard is it to clean? You can see the mess. Just clean it. Simple.*

I arrive on a Wednesday, grateful that Craig had closed the night before. He knows how to close! *Finally, an easy morning.*

The phone rings, and it's Melissa. Her car broke down and she can't close. No one in her family wants to pick her up at 3 am. *I don't blame them.*

"Come and work the day shift with me, and I'll see if Jesse, the other shift manager, can close." Now, I can have a sit-down chat with her about cleaning.

The shift is easy. Melissa is bubbly and great with customers and the team. After lunch, I grab my usual chicken burrito and ask Melissa to join me in the dining room. She pours a Pepsi and plops down.

"Hey, you are doing great. The team loves you, and you do great on speed. The one thing I need you to work on is cleanliness." I pull out the manager's log and show her all the notes and lists. She nods as if she gets it and promises to work on leaving the restaurant clean.

At 5 pm, we both end our shift. I can hear Melissa on the office phone.

"Hey. Yeah. Can you come and get me? I told you I was off at 5. It's not my fault the fucking car won't start." A pause.

"Screw you!" She slams the phone down.

She is in a bind, so I offer. "You need a ride?"

I can see the relief in her eyes. "Oh my God – if it's not too far. I have to get home by 6. My husband has to leave, and there's no one to watch my kids. And he won't come and get me."

We hop in my Honda Civic. I listen to Melissa chatter away. "Thank you so much. I need this job so badly. I like it, too, and I think I'm kind of good at it."

Except for CLEANING! I think to myself.

We arrive at her apartment in the city.

"Want to come up and meet my family?" she asks hopefully.

I hesitate for a moment. I'm not sure it is appropriate to go into a team member's home. Her request is sincere and warm, so I agree. We walk upstairs, down a dark hall, and into apartment 2B.

She announces our arrival. "I'm home."

A little person wearing only a diaper comes running and jumps into her arms. "Mama. Mama. Mama!"

As I enter her home, I am speechless and motionless. I am stunned by what I see. I force my legs to move into the living room, stepping over shoes, old newspapers, and a pile of mail.

"Come on in. Sit down. This is baby Bella." Melissa moves an empty pizza box and a dirty diaper to make room for me on the sofa. "I'm going to get a beer. Do you want one?"

I shake my head as she disappears into the kitchen with Bella on her hip. I slowly scan the room. Every flat surface is covered with dirty ashtrays, empty beer cans, and used plates. Heaps of dirty, or maybe clean, clothes are piled on the floor. The sofa and carpet are soiled. Through the open door to the kitchen, I spot an overflowing trash can. The sink and counter are piled high with dirty dishes. There is an empty Cheerios box in the baby's Pack'n Play.

Her husband hurries in and waves at me. "I'm Steve," he says as he rifles through the mound of clothes to find two matching socks. "I gotta go," he says as he pulls on the socks and his shoes, then rushes out the door.

I have a moment alone. Looking around, I am embarrassed. I am not embarrassed for Melissa as much as I'm ashamed of my ignorance and my assumptions.

When Melissa comes back into the living room, I make small talk for a few minutes.

"Hey, I need to head out. It was great to meet your family," I say as I give Bella's hand a little squeeze.

Melissa says, "Monica – thank you. Thanks for sticking with me."

Once in my car, it hits me. Of course, she can't clean the restaurant. I never showed her how. I never explained my expectations in detail. She has no frame of reference. I made huge assumptions based on my own experience. I made broad, general statements about keeping the restaurant clean. I never considered that she might have different standards or ideas.

After the visit to her apartment, I work several closing shifts with Melissa. Side-by-side, I show her what and how to clean. A few weeks later, we pass our food safety inspection. The team is so proud, and, late Sunday night, we have a great pizza party. I reward them all with new engraved name tags and new uniform shirts. I tell them, "A winning team deserves to look like winners."

■■■ Looking Back ■■■

I have often thought about Melissa and her apartment. Melissa taught me I couldn't assume that my team had the same experiences or priorities as I did. They didn't magically know the standards or my expectations. I certainly couldn't assume they knew the "how" and the "why" of the way we did things. I couldn't just write notes and make lists. I needed to show, teach, and coach them.

In the Army, we were taught "how" and "why" to do everything. Then, we repeated it over and over until it became a habit. Everyone made their bed the same way. We cleaned and maintained our weapons based on a standard. We had inspections in the Army, but I was never nervous about an inspection. I felt confident because the soldiers were trained. They knew what was expected. I needed the same approach for leading my restaurant team.

> I couldn't just write notes and make lists. I needed to show, teach, and coach them.

Saying "clean the restaurant" was not sufficient. I had to walk side-by-side with my team members and point out what was expected in detail. Often, that meant stating how the restaurant should be and how it should not be.

"The door thresholds need to shine. There should be no dirt in the little grooves."

"I expect clean tables. No sticky soda rings and no gum stuck underneath."

"There should not be one speck of dust on the top of the equipment."

This lesson went far beyond cleaning. So often throughout my career, we required team members to be "friendly," or to "treat the customers like family," or "welcome a customer like a guest in their home." Then, as the company, we evaluated our team members on whether they performed as we expected.

Team members have different backgrounds, come from different cultures, and have different

> If we want a certain performance, we must explain the behavior we want to see.

experiences. We assume that our team members' homes are friendly, inviting, clean, and safe. We can't assume we all agree on what "friendly" means. Words like "hospitality," "politeness," and "service" are vague concepts, not standards. If we want a certain performance, we must explain the behavior we want to see. Here are some examples:

- We don't keep customers waiting, ever. When a customer comes in, you stop what you are doing. You have five seconds to say "hello."
- When a customer comes in to order, you don't ask, "What do you want?" You ask, "How can I help you?"
- Every customer gets a "thank you."
- When a customer has a problem, you don't make them show you a receipt or show you the burrito to prove it was made wrong. You don't tell them that you did not do it. You say, "Let me fix that for you."

This lesson also applied to my management team. I would get so frustrated because of mistakes in counting cash or calculating inventory. I assumed that my managers could do basic math. Many couldn't. It was not their fault. I needed to teach them.

I got very good at this and codified it into a simple process to guarantee results:

Explain the standard – "This is what I expect."

Train the standard – Show them how to do it and explain why it's important.

Coach on the standard – Acknowledge progress and highlight places to improve.

Celebrate the successes – Behaviors that are recognized and celebrated are repeated.

If a team member could not perform to standard, I had to remove barriers that were making it difficult for them to perform. I had to make sure they had the tools they needed. And, I had to coach them. If they refused, I invited them to work somewhere else.

Lessons

- **Acknowledge different perspectives.** Each team member has a unique life experience different from yours. Don't assume that your understanding of a term is shared by your team.

- **Set high, specific standards.** No one will set a higher standard than you. Explain your expectations. Show your team what to do. Make sure your managers enforce the standards, too.

- **Explain, train, coach, and celebrate.** Use this simple process to get the performance you want.

7

SHAVING

*March 1994. Team Unit Manager, Taco Bell,
two restaurants in the Chicago suburbs*

I've been running two restaurants for three months now. Most days, it's just firefighting, racing back and forth while never getting ahead on important work, like hiring and training people.

My commute from home to the Berwyn restaurant is nearly an hour, so I have time to think and breathe. *Running two stores. Damn, this is hard. No wonder I'm so tired. Is this even possible? Project OOF really isn't going well. It's not just me. The other guys are struggling, too. Do these consultants know what they are doing? They believe that I can run two restaurants at the same time, but I don't know. The Army would never do this. Every platoon has its own leader.* I chuckle to myself as I imagine a poor lieutenant running across the tactical area, planning an assault with one platoon while the other platoon is calling on the radio. *No, the Army would never do this.*

Of course, this isn't war. It's business, and my results are a little better. The Westchester restaurant is doing okay, but sales are very soft. The location just doesn't bring the traffic we need. The Berwyn restaurant is much cleaner, and our labor is finally under control. For the first two months, we kept missing our labor target. We are only allowed to use a certain number of labor hours based on sales. Usually, Berwyn is allowed to use about 95 hours. If we use 97, we miss the labor target and have to make up two hours the next day. If sales are slow, we find out at the end of the day when the reports come out that we should have only used 90 instead of 95, so now we are down five hours. The problem is that we set the schedule ahead, and we won't know the sales numbers until the end of the day after the labor is already used. My assistant and I usually have to work an extra day at the end of the period to make up the hours we are over. Berwyn is consistently over on hours every day, an hour or two per day. Two weeks into the period we are over twenty hours. The boss starts calling.

Last month, I had a managers' meeting to get everyone together and explain the labor issue. The managers' meeting is a last resort because it also hurts labor. I must pay the shift managers to come to the meeting, which counts against the daily labor allotment.

"Guys, here's what we are allowed to use, and here –" I point to a line on a report, "– is what we are using. We are using too much!"

Craig blames me. "Everything was fine until we had to account for your hours."

"The labor tables are designed to include the manager's labor, so I am not the problem. We are simply using more than we are earning. So, you have to adjust, every shift. If sales are slow, then ask if anyone wants to go home. It's not hard during the evening shift. One of the high schoolers is always willing to go home early. Oh, and you have to give breaks! If they work five hours—"

"They don't want the damn breaks!" Craig grumbles loudly, interrupting me. "If they are scheduled for five hours, they don't want to clock out for thirty minutes!"

"Craig, it's the law. They have to take it, and it helps labor." I point out that if everyone takes a break, we can save two or three hours.

I go on to explain other ways to hit our labor targets. "Make sure they don't clock in early and don't stay late. We have to work together on this. It affects all our bonuses. Right now, we won't get our bonus if we don't fix the labor problem."

They look discouraged, and I realize I don't sound very encouraging, so I add, "We can do this! We can be a number one store in the market. Our cleanliness is really good now. Food cost is good, and you guys always have good sales numbers. Let's just get this labor thing under control."

For weeks, I drive hard on labor. I leave notes after every shift pointing out where a manager used too much labor. I call on my day off to check on how many hours we used. I scold. I threaten. I post signs. I sound like a broken record. "Labor, labor, labor."

It must be working, because we are getting better. The period ended last night, and we are actually three hours ahead without me needing to work an extra day. I guess I just needed to get everyone on the same page and nag a lot.

The hour commute goes by quickly. As I pull in, I am pleased with what I see. The parking lot is clean. Melissa is the opening manager, and I can tell she has done her manager's walk this morning. *Good job, Melissa.* I park in the furthest parking spot, saving the close spots for customers. As I stroll toward the entrance, I scan the ground. *She's really doing well. The lot looks clean, and the drive-thru window is spotless.*

Walking into the dining room, I can't help but smile. I closed last night, and, since I closed, I know that everything is clean and ready for today. I know the paperwork is filed and the office desk is clear. It was a long night, though. I finished up around 2:30 am. When I got to my car, I discovered that somebody had smeared bean burrito all over my windshield and car windows. It was probably one of the team members, pissed off because I make them keep the restaurant clean or take breaks. It could also have been an irate customer who ordered no cheese on his burrito and got cheese and decided to let me know how he felt. *Would have been nicer if he had just called the 1-800 number.* As if it wasn't bad enough to find beans smeared on every window, it was around 10 degrees outside and the beans had frozen. Turns out an ice scraper works on ice *and* frozen refried beans. By the time I got home, unwound, and fell asleep, it was probably 4 am. Short sleep.

As I step inside, Melissa greets me. "Hi! Welcome to your favorite Taco Bell," she says, poking at me. She knows that I run two stores and I can't play favorites. "I got the line set up, lot clean, deposits ready, and food safety check done."

"Hey, wow. Good job. Look at you! You're gonna be the restaurant manager before you know it. And great job making sure the lot has no litter!"

Melissa beams at the compliment.

"Oh, and did you see labor? We killed it," she exclaims.

"I did see the labor numbers, and you're right. For the first time in months, we made it. It will be nice not to get that call from Jason complaining about how we missed labor. Hey, you did such a great job on opening this morning. Do you want to run the deposit to the bank?"

"Yes!" She jumps at the chance. Going to the bank is a manager's privilege. It's fifteen minutes away from the restaurant and a chance to take a break, smoke a cigarette, or grab a coffee. Melissa knows I'm giving it up, my precious bank run.

She drives off to the bank, and I finish setting up the restaurant for opening: I open the registers, fill the ice machine, and check the prep schedule to make sure we have enough food ready for lunch.

Before I know it, Melissa is back. "Ahh – the joy of management." She tosses the bank receipt on the desk in the office. "Hey, have you had a chance to look at the time records? I think my pay was short again."

Melissa had complained about her pay a few weeks ago.

"Yes, I looked at the payroll report, and your check matched the time punches, so I don't see an issue." I am annoyed that she is asking again. The system is automated. *How could it be wrong?*

"Okay, but I don't know. It doesn't seem right, but hey, at least I got paid for driving to the bank," Melissa says as she puts a headset on and goes off to take our first order of the day.

Four weeks later, it's the end of the period, and labor is good. Food cost is good, and both restaurants have passed the Food Safety Audit. *My luck is changing!*

Today, I'm opening at Berwyn. I plop my stuff on the desk and then see the note in the manager's log.

I NEED TO TALK TO YOU. I'LL BE THERE TOMORROW MORNING AT 9:30.

MELISSA

Oh God. This can't be good. Please don't tell me you're quitting. I finally have you trained. Things are good. We have a steady team. Please don't quit. How will I cover your shifts?

I'm anxious. I have to recount the cash three times because all I can think about is Melissa's note. I don't have to wait long. Melissa is right on time.

"Let's sit in the dining room," she says, choosing a table far from the kitchen. She clearly doesn't want any other team members to hear our conversation. We sit down, and she opens her purse to take out a pile of small receipts.

"I've saved every one of these for the last two weeks," she says as she lays out the receipts. "They are my time punches. They show exactly when I punched in and when I punched out."

When a team member clocks in, the time clock prints out a little receipt. I have never seen anyone save the receipts. In fact, I always find them strewn around the front counter. Melissa has deliberately saved each one. She neatly lays out the stack, two receipts for each shift.

"I added all of these up. See?" She pulls out a yellow legal pad and shows me her clock-in and clock-out times for the entire pay period. "I added these up, and it doesn't match my pay."

She pulls out her pay stub, and she's right. The numbers don't match. She worked 79.45 hours but was only paid 77.85 hours – shorted over an hour and a half.

I study her pay stub and look at the little receipts. "I see what you are telling me, and I can't explain it. I will find out what's going on. There must be a mistake in the system or something. I'll find out. Can I have these?" I ask, pointing to the receipts and the yellow legal page.

She seems reluctant to give me her documents, but she agrees. "I have to go pick up the baby from my sister's. I'll see you tonight."

I thank her for coming in on her off time. I can't focus during lunch. *How could her pay be wrong?* I need to call Paul or Phil. They will help me figure this out. I really do appreciate these two. They are brothers, competitive and good at what they do.

"Paul? Hey. It's Monica."

"I know your voice, and, besides, my new office phone has a caller ID, so I can see who calls." Paul always has the latest technology and is good at the computer.

"Hey, one of my shift managers is complaining that she was shorted pay. When she first brought it up, I checked the labor report, and her paycheck matched. Then, today, she brought in the actual receipts from the time clock. She saved every time-punch receipt for the last two weeks and showed me. She was paid 1.6 hours less than she worked. How could that be?"

"Did you check the Time Punch Report for stars?"

"Did I what?"

"Ah, this could be – I'll come over and show you." Paul is running multiple stores, too, so for him to make time to come to my store is super helpful.

When Paul arrives, I'm waiting at a table in the dining room. He sits next to me and gets out a yellow highlighter. "Let's see the payroll report."

I slide it over to him. He takes one look and then begins highlighting line after line.

"What is it? What are you doing?"

After a minute, he shows me the report, filled with yellow lines. "See this little star at the end of the line? It means that the original time punch was changed. Come on –"

We head to the office computer, and Paul prints a report I have never seen: a Time Punch Change Report. "Just what I thought. Someone has been shaving hours. See, the system allows you to change a time punch."

"I know that," I say, a bit defensively. "Sometimes the kids forget to punch in or punch out, so I have to do it at the end of the day."

"Right! Exactly! That is why the system has this option to fix mistakes. Usually, you have a few changes a week. This report shows all the changes. It shows the original time punch and what it was changed to."

He hands me the report. I can't process what I'm seeing. There are dozens of lines. I see Melissa's name several times on the report and study the data.

> Original: 1700 - 0135
> Change: 1700 - 0130

Her time punch was changed, reduced by five minutes. She is not the only one.

"I don't get it. Why? Who?"

Paul frowns. "I've seen this before. Check the dates when the changes were made to see who was the closing manager."

I compare the report to the manager's schedule, and my heart sinks. Every night Craig closes, there are three or four changes to the time punches. Craig has been shaving a few minutes off employees' shifts to make up labor. The changes were so small that they didn't notice, except Melissa. Melissa noticed.

I look at Paul. "I have to call Jason."

Paul is sympathetic. "Monica. It's not your fault. Get ready, because it's probably been happening for months. They will audit and pay the team for any hours they were shorted. It will all hit your labor line. There goes your bonus."

Bonus? Who cares about a bonus? My team, my hard-working team, many of whom are barely making ends meet, are being cheated out of their wages. And this happened on my watch. I'm disgusted. I'm angry. *Why wasn't I ever told this could happen? Why do I have to learn everything the hard way?* I call Jason.

Jason and I meet with Craig the next day. Of course, Craig denies it. But the report doesn't lie. Then he blames the company for ridiculous targets and blames me for pushing them to hit the numbers and demanding that we use labor to clean the store.

I am disgusted by him. "You cheated the employees. You can't work for me."

Jason explains the termination to Craig, but I'm not listening. I'm thinking about all the doubles I have to work to cover Craig's shifts. I'm thinking about the bonus I won't get. I'm thinking about my team members. *This never should have happened.*

▪▪▪ Looking Back ▪▪▪

What my assistant manager did was wrong, and he was terminated. I wonder what pushed him to that point. When did he decide the only way that he could succeed was to compromise his integrity and cheat? And the real question is, what role did I play in this situation?

This experience taught me that there is a point, a breaking point, where pushing too hard to get results can push a team member over the edge. We seek to avoid pain and discomfort. If I created an environment that was so demanding that it created pain, I could expect some team members would find a way to stop that discomfort, even if it meant breaking the rules or compromising their integrity.

I wonder if I did enough to build capability to make sure my managers knew how to meet the labor targets. I also realize that I never explicitly said, "Do not cheat. Let's get results the right way." I never set that expectation. I just assumed that everyone would have the same principles that I had. By not spelling out the expectation, I may have inadvertently condoned cheating. The "get it done, I don't care how" mindset almost guarantees shortcuts and cheating. This experience taught me that I had to be very clear about my principles and "how" we get results.

Fear, intimidation, and constant pressure may get short-term results. It will almost always come at a cost. I have seen this throughout my career. I've seen managers pad their inventory when their food cost is too high. I've seen them game their customer feedback scores by having friends and family complete surveys. I've seen coaches push managers so hard that the managers postpone paying invoices until after the end of the bonus period. Fear-based leadership will result in low morale, unhealthy competition, high turnover, and, ultimately, someone will get fired because they couldn't find any way to avoid pain – and so, they cheat.

> **Fear, intimidation, and constant pressure may get short-term results. It will almost always come at a cost.**

After that incident and throughout my career, I tried to make clear and conscious choices about my messaging. I always wanted to get great results and make record profits. I wanted to be one of the best, but not through fear and intimidation. I would rather miss a target than have my team so afraid that they compromise their integrity. Even though not everyone agrees with this approach, that is how I chose to lead – the shadow I chose to cast.

The other lesson that this experience reinforced was to listen to my team. Melissa had told me weeks before that something was wrong. I dismissed her too quickly. I should have investigated more. It takes courage to come to a supervisor with an issue or problem. When someone on my team came to me, they knew that it was not just my door that was open, but also my ears and my mind.

Lastly, this experience taught me that some people will take the wrong path despite coaching and support. Craig was never on the same page as me. He resented that I was there, and when it got hard, he consciously made a terrible choice. At that point, my job was to solve the problem and make sure it never happened again.

Lessons

- **Using fear and intimidation to get results will come at a cost.** Your team will find a way, and it will likely compromise what they believe is right. Decide how you want to lead, and be clear about how you want to get results.

- **Listen to the team and take their concerns seriously.** This is a vital part of your job as their leader.

- **Some people on your team will make bad choices.** It's not about you. Take appropriate action, and move on.

8

GOOD OR BAD –
WHO'S TO SAY?

December 1994. End of my career as a Team Unit Manager

It's been several months since we terminated Craig for shaving hours. I promote one of my shift managers to assistant manager and train a team member to take his place. Finally, I have a full management staff at both restaurants. I've been running two restaurants for about a year. They want me to take on a third, but I can't. *I won't.* This multi-unit manager is going to stop at two, especially since both restaurants are finally at a place where I can take a break.

I can't remember the last time I took a real vacation. It must have been when I was still in the Army. Yeah, it was probably when I took ten days leave from my tour in Korea and went to Thailand and Indonesia. What an adventure, but damn, that was four, maybe five years ago. No wonder I'm so tired. I need this vacation so badly. I can't wait to get on that plane, order a beer, and leave all my worries in Chicago. Hopefully, my assistant managers won't screw it up too much. I spent the last two weeks getting them ready for me to be away.

"Daryl, I did the schedule, so all you have to do are four simple things. Place the food order on Tuesday. Get the money to the bank – you do that every day. Enter correct inventory counts every night, and, for God's sake, call in the numbers to Jason every morning by 9. If you don't call in the numbers, I'm going to get a phone call, and I really don't want a phone call on vacation. You remember which numbers? Sales, labor, food, and speed. Got it? Here on the clipboard – here is everything I just said. Okay?"

Daryl rolls his eyes and nods his head. Then he repeatedly points to his headset earpiece, the universal fast-food symbol for "I can't listen to you anymore. I have a customer."

I roll my eyes and wonder if he even has a customer at the drive-thru menu board. Maybe I have gone overboard on nagging them. It's near the end of the bonus cycle, and I really don't need a bad week to screw my bonus check. *OMG – I forgot.* Rushing to the front, I call, "Daryl! Daryl! DON'T FORGET ABOUT DAILY FOOD SAFETY. Keep the blue towels in the blue buckets. Make sure the cold line stays cold and the sanitizer –"

He whirls around, glares at me, and says into his headset mic, "I'm sorry, sir. My manager is a raving maniac, and I couldn't hear you. Could you repeat your order?"

I stop my food safety laundry list and stare at him. "You don't have a customer."

"Yes, I do!" He pushes the microphone button to tell the customer to "please pull around to the window."

"Very funny. Not!" I glare, knowing the customer did not hear him call me crazy.

After he hands out the order, he slowly turns and looks at me. "Seriously? I've been doing this for three years. We have never failed a food safety audit, and we are not going to fail on my watch. It's my bonus too, ya know?"

"Sorry," I mumble. "You're right." The truth is that Daryl is ready to be promoted to restaurant manager, and, as soon as a restaurant is open, I will probably lose my assistant. Good for him. Bad for me.

"Go to Colorado. See your family. Have fun, and don't worry about this place, or food costs, or food safety. We got this!"

I smile at him. "Thanks. I'll see you in a week. Call if you need me."

Even though I say it, I pray he doesn't. I really, really need a break from this place. Twelve-hour shifts and running two restaurants have exhausted me.

Once on the plane, I settle in and dream about the upcoming trip. I will see my family and all my old softball buddies. It will feel good to just kick back, have some beers, and do a little skiing. I drift off to sleep and wake as the plane touches down in Denver.

Within hours, I'm at the bar with my old crew sucking down Coors Light. They want to hear all about my life in Chicago, and then they come – the questions about my job. I have to explain to my friends that I'm a fast-food restaurant manager. They don't mean to judge, but I can hear it in the tone of their questions.

"Wait – you actually work in a Taco Bell? In a Taco Bell?"

"Yes. I actually work in a Taco Bell, well – two Taco Bells right now."

The grilling continues.

"Is the meat real meat?"

"Do you guys spit in the food? "

"Why can't you ever get my order right when I order my burrito with no sour cream?"

I wish I could explain to them how hard the job is and how I manage two million-dollar businesses with fifty employees. I wish they could see how seriously we take food safety and how we hate it when we screw up their orders, but I'm too tired to explain.

"Whatever. You guys suck. Yes, it is real beef. Give me another beer."

Hope was one of my closest Colorado buddies. We were in the Army together at Fort Carson in Colorado Springs. We played softball, went to bars in Denver, and looked out for each other. She looks at me with concern and asks some legit questions. "You look beat. Are you having fun? Why do you work there? Didn't all the other former junior military officers quit?"

"Yeah, most of the other guys are gone. They were engineers and went to other companies. I guess I stay because I don't know what else I would do. And I don't want to quit until I figure it out."

"Buddy, it shouldn't be this hard. Think about it." Hope is wise, and I do think about it, but I don't have the energy to look for another job. *Screw it. Right now, I'm on vacation.*

The next morning, we hit the ski slopes. It has been several years since I donned skis, and, even though I am not in very good shape, when I hop on the ski lift, I feel alive. The cold, fresh, mountain air clears my head. My restaurant worries fade. The "Rocky Mountain high" is real, and I gulp its energy into my depleted spirit. *Freedom is not having to worry about food safety!*

I take an easy green on my first run and rediscover how beautiful a snow-covered mountain looks and feels beneath my skis. I gently swish back and forth down the gradual trail back to the lift.

On the second run, I choose another green trail. About a third of the way down, I pause to wait for my sister, Meg. The next thing I know, I am on my butt. This old guy had skied past me. He wasn't going fast, but, somehow, our skis got tangled and I fell. I fell and felt the "pop." Sitting on the slope, I grab my right knee. The pain is immediate but not unbearable.

A woman skiing by looks at me and stops. She expertly pops off her skis and squats down next to me. "Well, we might as well get this started now."

She packs snow around my knee and tells me to wait for the ski rescue. She knows. She knows what I don't.

The ski patrol guy arrives and straps me into a sled. The ride down should be fun, but I have a sense of dread. The ski patrol guy knows, too. He suggests that I go to the local clinic and have my knee checked out. There, I learn my fate: it is very likely that I tore my ACL. The ski resort clinic doctor knows what that means. It will be a few days before I understand the magnitude of my injury.

I spend the remainder of my vacation drinking with my buddies, icing my knee, and feeling sorry for myself. *Why me? On the second run? Who gets injured skiing while they are standing still? Sucks.*

Back in Chicago, the orthopedic doctor confirms it. "You have a torn ACL. That's the anterior cruciate ligament. It holds you upright. Your only decision is pig, or cadaver, or your own tissue."

I blink rapidly as I try to understand what this doctor just said. "Um – what? What are you talking about?"

He takes a deep, slightly irritated breath and spells it out in language I can grasp. "You need surgery. I have to re-build your ligament. I can use a tissue harvested from a deceased person's knee. Or, I can use tissue from a pig. Or, I can take part of your patellar tendon and carve a new ligament from your own tissue. I'll screw the new ligament into the bone, and, after some time, you should have full use of your knee for many years to come."

"After some time?" I ask in panic and dread.

"It can take up to a year to fully recover, but you will be walking the same day. In fact, you will walk out of the clinic a few hours after surgery and need crutches for a few days. Then, you'll start rehab."

I breathe a sigh of relief. I had imagined the worst, unable to walk for days and needing crutches. "Oh, thank God. I thought I would have to miss weeks of work. It sounds like I can return to work soon after surgery."

"What do you do?" Dr. Fields asks.

"I am a restaurant manager for Taco Bell."

"Oh, no way!" He laughs while saying it. "I'm not releasing you to work in a RESTAURANT. One slip on a greasy floor and you could tear the new ligament I just made. No, you will have to clear physical therapy before getting a release."

The panic returns, as do tears. "How – how long? How long does that usually take?"

He shrugs his shoulders. "It depends on your recovery."

Back in Chicago, I have a hectic week preparing for surgery. There is insurance paperwork, travel plans for my parents, and, most importantly, my call to Jason, my boss.

"Yeah, the surgery is Tuesday. They have to build a new ligament. I don't know when they will release me to come back, maybe a week. I'll call you as soon as I know. How are the restaurants? Did we make labor while I was out?"

Jason is kind and reassuring. He tells me not to worry about the restaurants. "Have the surgery, and then let's figure out next steps. Just take care of yourself."

Surgery day, I'm lying on a cold table. Waiting. The lights in the operating room are blindingly bright. There is so much activity – bags of fluid hang next to me, needles in my arm. Waiting, I wonder if the restaurants got their food delivery on time and if everyone showed up for lunch shift.

The doctor comes in with a Sharpie marker. "Right knee? Yes?"

I nod as he puts a huge "X" on my left knee. In this case, I guess X means "wrong way," not like "X marks the spot." I had not thought to worry about surgery on the wrong knee. *What else should I be worrying about?*

Anesthesia is weird. You count backward from ten, and, the next thing you know, you are groggily waking up in a recovery room. The doctor walks in with my parents and proudly announces that the surgery was a huge success. I had chosen to use my own tissue. Dead guy tissue in my knee was too weird.

"You had great tissue to harvest, and the screws went in perfectly. I'll write a script for pain medication and physical therapy. A nurse will come by to explain the rest. See you in a month." And, off he goes to make more ligaments.

I try to focus my still-drowsy eyes. "Hi, what time is it?"

Dad answers. "It's 1:30. The surgery only took a few hours. This is amazing! Your doctor is phenomenal. He came out during surgery and showed us this picture of your knee. See – here is the old torn part, and here is the new part that he made."

"Dad, I can't. Not now. I need to know what's going to happen to me."

I push the X-ray or MRI or whatever it is away and wait for the nurse. When the nurse arrives, I anxiously ask, "How soon—?"

Before I can finish, she says, "Let's start at the beginning. We are working up the discharge papers. This afternoon, a therapist will come to your home to set up a machine to move the knee. Stay on the machine as much as possible. Blood flow will help the new ligament. By tomorrow, you will start to feel some pain, so use the pain medicine and take all the antibiotics. You should walk with crutches for a few days, and make an appointment for your first physical therapy. They will explain how you will regain full movement and strength. Any questions?"

I have a lot of questions but the most burning one is, "When can I go back to work? I'm a restaurant manager. Well, actually, I manage two restaurants. When can I go back to work?"

She looks at me with compassion and says gently, "You just had major surgery to repair your knee. Your most important job this week is to manage the swelling and pain. And to get that knee moving. The physical therapist will explain recovery."

"I have to tell my company something. WHEN? When can I go back to my restaurant?"

"It's hard to say, but you can probably drive in a few—"

"I can't drive? Please, you have an idea. Give me a ballpark. What are we looking at? I still have ten days of vacation, so a week or two is okay. Please!"

"You literally work in a restaurant, a fast-food restaurant?" she asks, shaking her head. "Look, if you had an office job, you could return to work in a few weeks. But a restaurant? You are probably looking at around twelve weeks before the ligament is strong enough."

My world stops. I see, hear, and feel nothing. Twelve weeks? Three months? I can't be gone for three months. They won't leave my restaurants without a manager for three months. How will I pay my bills? What will happen to me back at home, strapped into the knee machine? I am genuinely afraid for my future and my career. I can't move back in with my parents. I can't be unemployed. I have a mortgage and a car payment on a car I can't drive. It's terrible luck. To have worked this hard, injure my knee on vacation, have a painful surgery and recovery, and now lose my job?

The next day, I call Jason. "Hey, thanks for the balloons and flowers. That was really nice."

"Well, we missed you yesterday at the meeting. Everyone was asking about how you are doing."

"I'm doing okay. The surgery went well, and the pain is not too bad. I start physical therapy tomorrow. I have therapy three times a week, and my friends said they will drive me. But, here's the thing. The surgical nurse said it could be twelve weeks before I can work – but it could be sooner!" I try to sound optimistic. "I'm so sorry. I will try to get back as soon as I can."

I hear the kindness in his voice as he says, "Monica, you had a bad accident. It's not your fault. Never say you're sorry. We will be fine. The restaurants will be fine. Your job right now is to heal and get strong. Don't worry about work. We will be here when you are ready."

"But who will run the restaurants? And how will I afford to live? I can't miss six paychecks!"

"Relax! I'll take care of the restaurants. As far as your pay, I called in your LOA, and you're on a medical leave of absence. Since you also elected disability insurance, you will get eighty percent of your pay while you are out on leave. You'll be okay."

"Wait, I'll get paid most of my salary while I'm out?"

"Yes, so work hard to get better. Don't worry about the restaurants. I don't even want you to call the restaurants. Hear me? Get strong, and we will see you in a few months."

As I hang up the phone, I feel two things: intense relief and immense gratitude. I won't be fired.

Recovery begins. Three times a week, my friend Tammy drives me to the center where I re-learn to balance on the injured leg and do squats and step-ups. Progress is slow. Sometimes, it is painful. Full-time recovery is my job now. I have nothing else to do. I'm not permitted to call my restaurants, and I can't exactly ride a bike or go dancing. So, I sit, ice my knee, and reflect on the last few years.

What am I doing? Is this what I'm supposed to be doing? What else would I do? I like to write. Maybe I could be a writer. Maybe I could get promoted and do writing for work?

Jason told me to "get strong." He meant physically. My knee is getting stronger and so are my mind and heart. I am not exhausted or stressed. I am focused and calm. I decide that I want to study writing and I find a Master of Science in Written Communication at the National University in Evanston. Classes are once a week. Maybe Taco Bell will let me off a little early to go to class. I enjoy the application process, and, for the first time in a long time, I am hopeful and excited.

The twelve weeks do not go by quickly or slowly, but the ski accident and all my bad luck seem like a long time ago. What I thought was so terrible has not been so bad. The time off gives me perspective and time to rest. I feel like a different person.

The day finally arrives. I am clear to return to work. My knee is strong, and so is my heart. I lost fifteen pounds and smoke a lot less. Time to get back to work.

I call my buddy Paul to get the gossip. "Hi, Paul. What's going on?"

"Hey, we heard you're coming back tomorrow. You missed a lot!"

"Oh?" I'm curious but not surprised. I was gone for a long time.

"Yeah, they had a big meeting about OOF, and they decided to end it. They ended OOF!"

Now I'm surprised. No, I'm stunned. "Really? Organization of the Future is over?"

Paul continues his update. "Yeah, turns out they realized every store needs an RGM. Shoot, I could have told them that, and they could have given me all that money they paid the consultants." He laughs.

"Wow, so what's happening?"

"Well, they are taking everybody down to one restaurant. They promoted a bunch of assistants and brought on a few new guys. I'm keeping Naperville. Daryl got promoted to run Westchester, and a new guy got Berwyn."

I inhale deeply. Both of my restaurants have new leaders. I had heard that Daryl got promoted while I was on leave. I am happy for him. He deserves to be a restaurant manager. I am surprised to hear that my other store also has a new manager. I feel my stomach knot. I exhale slowly. "Where will I go?"

Paul says he doesn't know, but I bet he does. He knows everything. I'll know tomorrow, and that feels like forever.

The next morning, Jason and I meet at the office and he greets me. "It's so great to have you back. How do you feel?"

"Thanks. I feel very good. And thanks, too, for all the support. Everyone was so helpful. Really, Jason, thank you."

"Of course. So, a lot happened while you were gone. We ended the OOF experiment, so now every restaurant will have a manager. Let's talk about what's next for you. I think you're going to really like this."

We pour ourselves coffee and settle into chairs in a conference room.

He continues. "We are giving you Glendale Heights."

"What? Wait – what? That restaurant is like a half mile from my house. Really? Seriously? That is fantastic. I won't have to drive for almost an hour to get to my restaurant. Wow!"

"Right, this should be a much easier commute. The restaurant has a stable team, and Johnny is a great assistant manager. In fact, he could be a restaurant manager, but he doesn't want it."

"This is unbelievable. I am so excited."

"There is one more thing. We want you to get certi-fied to become a Restaurant Training Manager so you can train other new managers. We have watched you for the last couple years and think you will be a great trainer. Of course, your restaurant must perform at a high level, but Johnny will help with that. Oh, and you get a raise once you get certified to train. So, what do you think?"

Three months ago, I sat on a mountain, injured and scared. Today, I am strong and healthy. Today, I learn that the company recognizes me as a good trainer and that it is giving me the restaurant closest to my house. Plus, I get a raise? I'm speechless, until I realize that Jason is waiting for an answer.

I smile widely and nod. "What do I think? What do I think? I think *yes*! One hundred percent, *yes*!"

■■■ Looking Back ■■■

There is an old Chinese parable about a farmer, his son, and a horse.

One day, a farmer's horse runs away. The villagers feel bad for the farmer and say to him, "We heard the bad news. What will you do? How will you farm since your horse ran away?"

The farmer says, "Good or bad. Who is to say?"

A few weeks later, the horse returns to the farm with two wild horses following. The villagers congratulate the farmer. "What good luck! Now you have three horses."

The farmer says, "Good or bad. Who is to say?"

While breaking in one of the wild horses, the man's son is thrown off and badly injures his leg. The villagers console the farmer.

"What a terrible loss. How can you work the farm without your son's help?"

Again, the farmer says, "Good or bad. Who is to say?"

A war breaks out in the country, and all the young men go off to war. Many are injured. Many die. The farmer's son did not have to go because of his leg injury. The villagers say to the farmer, "You are so lucky that your son did not have to fight."

"Good or bad. Who is to say?"

At the time, the ski accident seemed like terrible luck. I was injured, alone, and afraid of losing my job. I was discouraged and angry. It was a "bad" thing. Looking back, it was the catalyst for one of the biggest changes in my life. Yes, it was a hard experience, but it also provided me the space to assess my choices and how I was living my life. It gave the company time to think about how my skills were best utilized. I ended up becoming a training manager at a restaurant very close to my home. Imagine being so close that I could watch my drive-thru lane from the treadmill at Bally's Gym across the street.

"Good or bad. Who is to say?"

Good or bad. Who's to say? The lesson is perseverance and resilience. I remember this sign I once saw in a therapist's office.

It will be okay in the end. If it is not okay, it's not the end.

The other thing I learned from the ski accident is that my company and my coach were there when I needed them. They supported me during a challenging time. They never made me feel bad about being out for three months.

Rather, they did everything they could to make recovering from my accident easy.

Throughout my career, when someone would get injured or had to support a sick family member, I recalled my knee injury. I remembered how scared I was that I would lose my job or fall out of favor with my boss. Things happen to people, and that is when

> It will be okay in the end. If it is not okay, it's not the end.

they most need our care and support. They need to know we have their backs and will be there for them when they are ready. Often (though not always), the payoff for loyalty is loyalty.

Lessons

- **Good or bad – who's to say?** Adversity will happen, but you never know how things will turn out. Stay focused. Be positive. Trust that the best is yet to come.

- **Be kind to your people when they are experiencing hardship.** Give them as much leeway as possible. One day, it might be you. Loyalty is a two-way street. When you support your team during hard times, they will be there for you, often tenfold.

9

IT'S NOT ABOUT THE TACOS

April 1995. Restaurant General Manager, Taco Bell,
Glendale Heights, Illinois

My new restaurant is less than one mile from my house.
It's a mission-style Taco Bell, old but in good condition.
The business is strong, and the team is amazing. They are
a diverse group who enjoy each other's company. The best
part about Glendale Heights is Johnny, the assistant manager. He is the calmest, most capable assistant manager I've
ever met. I'm determined to keep my newfound balance
and sense of peace. Johnny is the perfect role model. He
is gentle but firm with the team, follows all the standards,
and is delightful to the guests. He takes care of inventory,
cleaning, and maintenance. When the unexpected happens,
he just calmly deals with the situation. If someone doesn't
show for their shift, or the truck is late, he does the best he
can without exerting a bunch of stress-filled energy.

After a few weeks at the new restaurant, Jason starts
the process to certify me as a training manager. It is easy.

I have to go to a class or two and pass a test to prove that I can "train." The restaurant has to pass an inspection to prove it is ready to host trainees. The only open switch is convincing my managers that becoming a training restaurant is a good idea. I scheduled a meeting.

"So, you all know that we are working to become a training restaurant. Right? Well, I heard you have some questions. So, let's talk about it." I really do want to hear their concerns.

"Why? Why do we want the extra work?" asks Anthony, one of the shift managers.

"What extra work? You already run an exceptional restaurant. Glendale Heights is one of the best restaurants in the market. We hit all the numbers, pass inspections, and have great customer scores. Our restaurant is a great place for new managers to learn."

I sense this explanation isn't winning their support, so I try another approach. "There are benefits, like extra labor. Corporate will give us extra labor hours so that I can spend time with the trainees. Plus, even though the trainees 'work' in our restaurant, we don't have to pay their salary. Corporate does, so it's kind of like free labor."

I smile, because now I have their attention. "But remember, just because we have a manager trainee doesn't mean we can use them like a team member. All of us are going to have to help the trainees. We want trainees who come from Glendale Heights Training Restaurant to be capable of running shifts, right?"

They nod silently in agreement. I think the extra labor has them convinced.

"There's one more thing. We have to tighten up our procedures a bit. We are an excellent restaurant, but we have to go by the book. No shortcuts! The trainees will read the manuals and learn how to do things properly. They must see the same thing in our restaurant."

"Does this mean we can't break down the line early?" asks Wael, one of the shift managers.

I wince. That is a hard one. We all break down the line an hour before closing so we can wash all the dishes and get out at 1 am instead of 2:30 am. It's an unauthorized shortcut. We swap out all the dirty pans for clean ones, clean the line, and put plastic on it so that we can just do a quick wipe down at closing. We keep the hot food hot and have all the products available until closing time, but it's still against the policy.

I hesitate a minute and say, "The trainees won't close every night, and, when they do, I will work with them. But everything else – the razor blades, cutting tomatoes with a knife instead of using the slicer, skipping olives on the pizzas – all that has to change. So, do we agree? We will use safety gloves, pink safety box cutters, and suggestive sell during rush, even though it slows us down. OK?"

Long pause. I look at Johnny. He loves his razor blades for cutting the flaps off boxes. And much of my work will fall on him if I become a training manager. Johnny nods his head and says in a whisper, "I will keep it in my car."

I smile and look around. They all nod, and Wael says, "Okay, we will do it – at least when the trainee is around!"

They all giggle, and the meeting ends.

Every few weeks, we are assigned a new manager trainee. The team enjoys getting to know the trainees and helping with the training. But no one is enjoying the training more than I am. I usually arrive at the restaurant an hour before the trainee, so I can check the numbers and inspect the restaurant. Johnny does a great job, and every-thing looks great. My time with the trainees is easy and fun. *Is that the right word? Fun? At work?*

The best part is watching the new person become con-fident in running a shift in a restaurant. I'm proud of the leaders I am training, and I'm relaxed. I even start taking classes to get my graduate degree. Jason is accommodating when I leave early on Wednesdays, so I can be at class on time. And bonus! I had no idea that Taco Bell has a tuition reimbursement program to pay for it – so it's free! *Is life really this good?*

Today is a rare day on which I don't have a trainee, and I'm looking forward to spending some dedicated time with my high school kids. They stroll in around 4 pm, drop their backpacks in the tiny employee area, grab a free-for-employees Pepsi, and chat me up.

"Hey Monica, what's going on?"

"Monica, where am I working tonight?"

"Where are the trainees?"

"Where are the extra name tags?"

"Who is the closing manager?"

The last question always makes me smile because I used to do the same thing when I was sixteen. I got my first job at Chuck E. Cheese and loved working there once I figured out how to get out of the costume. Like most new hires, I started out dressing up in the stinky Chuck costume. Kids pulled my tail and yelled in my face. The costume was hot and sweaty and reeked of body odor. Those were long four-hour shifts.

I was a quick new hire, though. I figured out that if I learned to make pizzas and was fast about it, I could get out of the costume and work in the kitchen with the "cool kids." I was out of that costume in two weeks and one of the fastest on the pizza-making line. Plus, I showed up on time, which earned me cred with the cool kids.

Soon, I was trained to close. This meant longer shifts, working late at night, and sneaking beers in the parking lot after close. I loved closing shift, but it all depended on who was the closing manager. Rita sat in her office and talked to her boyfriend on the phone. Easy! Jim was the big boss. He never checked up on us. He was always looking at reports. But DeeDee – she was the tough one. She would run her hands along the top of equipment to make sure it was clean. She would feel under the cooler handles, checking for caked-on pizza sauce. I had to work harder to pass DeeDee's inspections. So, way back then, when I clocked in for my shift, the first thing I would say was, "Who's closing?" Just like my kids today!

I answer their barrage of questions. "Nothing is going on. We don't have a new trainee until tomorrow. Check the deployment board for your assignment. Spare name tags are on the shelf in the office, and Wael is closing."

I am sure they are less than pleased because he is like DeeDee – tough. Wael has just passed his shift manager certification and is working hard to run great shifts. As they take their positions and continue their banter, I notice that Khalil is unusually quiet.

"Hey, what's going on with you?" I ask.

"Nothing."

Wael chimes in. "He's nervous about an algebra test. He thinks he's not going to pass, and he probably won't."

They all cackle at Khalil's misery with math.

"Algebra?" I ask. "Like quadratic equations?"

They abruptly stop what they are doing and stare at me.

"You know algebra?" Khalil asks incredulously.

"You guys! I went to college! Yes, I know algebra, chemistry, physics, and calculus. I have a degree in Biology."

"YOU DO?" Wael asks in utter shock.

I guess I never talk about my education, and they assume that the restaurant manager must be, well – not educated.

"Khalil, my shift ends at 8 pm. How about we sit in the dining room and see if we can figure out how to solve for "x" to help you pass that test?"

As we sit together and work through algebra problems, I realize, maybe for the first time, that I am helping one of my team members in a way I'd never imagined. It feels odd, but good. His education has nothing to do with working in my restaurant, and yet, somehow, it feels like this is part of my job. It is uniquely mine to do, and I like it – a lot.

"Hey, I can meet you here tomorrow night to do more studying, if you want," I offer. "Let's make sure you are really ready for your test on Friday."

A week later, Khalil comes bounding in to his work shift and proudly shows me his paper. He passed his algebra test! Soon after Khalil's test, other kids start asking for help. I am proofreading papers and helping with chemistry.

One afternoon, Eva comes in distressed. She opens her backpack, pulls out a thick pile of papers, and goes off. "I can't figure this out. It's so confusing. There are so many forms and things I have to do. My parents can't help me, 'cause they don't know English. It's just not fair."

"Hey, hey – slow down. What's all this?" I ask.

"It's for college. I need to do all this so I can go to college, and it's so much, and there are deadlines."

"Hey, we got this. You just need a system. Come on. It's slow right now. Let's go out to the dining room. Bring all that stuff, and let's go through it."

Thirty minutes later, we have organized all the paperwork into piles. We create a little spreadsheet so Eva can track due dates for essays, applications, and fee schedules. She is much calmer now that she has a plan. Me? I feel calm, too, maybe even happy. Even though helping a kid get into school isn't my job, it feels really good. My boss will never know. It won't increase my bonus. It won't help me pass my audits. Yet, I like how it makes me feel. I helped someone within the construct of my job, and I want to do more of it because, well – I like it. I guess Jason was right. I am a pretty good trainer and coach.

▪▪▪ Looking Back ▪▪▪

That was thirty years ago, and I often wonder what happened to my old team. Was I remembering this correctly? Did it really happen like I remember? *What would those team members say now, after thirty years?*

I decided to look up Khalil on social media. He still lives in Chicago and has a wife and two kids. He went to college and got a degree in Computer Software and Media Applications. He can probably do way more than algebra now! As I read on, I learned that he is a seasoned restaurant leader. At one time, he managed over forty restaurants, receiving high awards for leadership. *Wow! That was my high school kid, and now he is a leader in the industry. I wonder what he remembers from those early days.*

So, I messaged Khalil and asked him what he remembers about our days together at Glendale Heights Taco Bell. He replied,

> *"I recall how you and Johnny took me under your wing, nurturing me into the role of shift leader. I had arrived in this country without any experience, English proficiency, or management skills. Gradually, both you and Johnny motivated me to learn and grow. Our location was bustling with trainees to guide, yet you managed to both develop the staff and meet the demands of the business. I remember vividly watching you on the line, side by side, assembling tacos. You dedicated a significant amount of time to Johnny's development as well. The culture from that time remains dear to my heart, and those days are still fresh in my memory."*

This! This is what it is about. It was never about the tacos, burritos, food safety, or labor costs. It seems obvious to me now, but back then I had to discover that my role as a leader wasn't to run around stressed out while trying to pass audits.

My job was to help people: customers and trainees, and, most of all, my team. It wasn't about me. It was about them.

The beautiful part of this discovery is that it felt good – really good. Brian Bosche, owner and CEO of The Purpose Company and co-author of *The Purpose Factor*, calls this "fulfillment." He says,

My job was to help people: customers and trainees, and, most of all, my team. It wasn't about me. It was about them.

"Fulfillment is using the best of what you have to help others." That is the feeling. It's fulfillment.

Lessons

- **Find fulfillment in your role as a leader by helping others.** You have something to give to your team members that can change the trajectory of their lives.

- **Be a role model.** Teachers and coaches impact lives. So do managers. Your team members watch you. They listen to you. They look up to you. They will emulate you.

- **Be the first boss who makes a lifelong, positive impact.** Everyone remembers their first boss. That young person who starts for you today? You are their "first boss." Be a boss who inspires them to achieve their potential, challenges them to learn and grow, and believes in them.

10

BE LIKE SANDI

Fall of 1995. Restaurant Training Manager, Taco Bell, Glendale Heights, Illinois

I'm beyond excited. Corporate is coming all the way from Irvine, California, to Chicago. Out of the 5,000 restaurants in the country, they are coming to my restaurant – mine! These are the visits that shape careers (or kill them). I'll meet the bigwigs. I can show off my team. I can tell them everything – all the things that they need to do to make it easier for managers like me to run better restaurants.

The corporate visit is all I think about. I spend weeks preparing. I don't have much in my budget for maintenance, so I make the most out of the little I have. My restaurant is old, and there is much to repair. I hire a handyman to replace the broken ceiling tiles and replace the men's room mirror for the seventh time. The etched FU won't be a good look. To spruce up the landscaping, I plant flowers myself. I schedule all the cleaning tasks and order new shirts. I don't have the budget to buy new shirts for every team member in the restaurant, but I will be able to hand out new shirts to the team who will work that day. I order new white trash bins; clean white bins signal a sparkly-clean restaurant. I close the night before the big visit so I can ensure that everything is cleaned and organized for the next day. My team knows I am excited. They are working extra hard. I finish my closing paperwork so I can help them. Mo is scrubbing the grout, and I take on polishing the door thresholds. The last thing to do is paint over the scuff marks on the walls. I hide the paint cans in my car since paint is not an approved chemical. Having an unapproved chemical in the restaurant could cause us to fail a surprise inspection. I meticulously paint over every last black mark. The beige walls look perfect. We are ready.

There's much to do in the morning to prepare for the big visit. I'm fourth on the tour, so they will likely arrive at my restaurant around 1 pm. I'm told the group includes the chief people officer, senior director of training, and a few others from the training department. I'm so excited to talk to this group from corporate because there is a lot that they could do to improve the training materials. In my spare time, I'm working on that Master of Science in Written Communication and have a lot of passion for great instructional design. *Hope they want to hear my ideas.*

The morning flies by, and I'm excited and nervous. Rocio, my cashier, calmly reassures me, "It's okay, Monica. We got you."

And they do. Rocio has the other team members pumped up, too. I'm sure she told them to be extra friendly to the customers. Like me, she is proud of our restaurant and wants to impress the VIPs from California. The team looks great in their new uniform shirts, and everyone remembered their name tags. I had replaced their label-maker name tags and splurged on new engraved name tags. *They really do look good.*

Lunch rush at 1 pm is not an ideal time for them to arrive at my restaurant, so it might be hard to spend time with them if we are super busy. Around 10 am, I call my buddy Ray in the next suburb. He's first on the list.

"Are they there yet?" I ask.

"Nope, I heard they are having a meeting first."

"Okay, well, call me when they pull in your lot. Okay? You promised!" Ray is an old-time manager who can run the heck out of his restaurant.

I can tell he is nervous that they might come at lunch.

"I just want to get this over with and run my store," he says.

I reassure him that he is going to be okay. I call him again at 11 am and 11:30 am. There is still no sign of the van full of big corporate leaders from California.

"Don't call me during rush," Ray says.

"I know, I know –" *I'm not stupid.*

Lunch is particularly busy, and I'm distracted scanning the parking lot for a van. As soon as lunch is over, I rally the team to get the restaurant cleaned up and restocked so we are ready for our guests.

The store phone rings, and it's Sarah, the manager whose restaurant is after me on the tour. "Have they come by?"

"Nope, Ray said he would call me when they hit his lot." I glance at my watch. *Holy shit – it's 1:30 already.* "I will call you when they get here."

Sarah sighs and hangs up. She's nervous too.

The team recovers from lunch, and I start sending them on breaks. Around 3 pm, I realize I'm starving because I've only had a few cups of coffee. My standby, a chicken burrito steamed in the pizza melter, is warm and gooey and comforting.

At 4 pm, Ray calls me. "They ain't coming."

I breathe a heavy sigh. "You might be right." *Damn it. Corporate losers – liars.*

Rocio comes to me with a concerned look. "Monica, I have to go. I'm sorry. I can't stay and wait any longer."

"I know, Rocio. Thank you for everything you did." She's disappointed. I am too. But even if she could stay, I don't have the budget for overtime. "I'll see you tomorrow!" *I love her.*

Johnny arrives at 5 pm for his closing shift. He sees my face and immediately thinks we blew the visit. "It was bad?" he asks.

"No, they never showed, but at least you will have an easy close. The restaurant is spotless."

At 6:30 pm, I am packing my stuff when the phone rings. It's Ray. "They just pulled into my lot."

At 7:30 pm, they arrive at my restaurant. I have been on my feet for over thirteen hours. I'm exhausted. My night crew doesn't have nice new shirts and Rocio is long gone, but the VIPs are here. I meet Connie, Mike, and Sandi. Despite the late hour, they are enthusiastic and curious. They ask me a ton of questions. "Tell us about your restaurant. How long have you been here? What is the sales volume? How many team members do you have?"

I beam with pride as I brag about my team and our restaurant. I catch Johnny out of the corner of my eye. He's smiling.

Sandi asks the next question. "What do you think of the training programs?"

This. This is the question. I pause. I have been waiting for this question. The other restaurant managers have warned me not to say anything bad about Corporate, even if they ask. "Just tell them everything is okay. It could kill any hope of promotion if you complain about something." I have argued with them that things can't get better if we don't tell the leaders who can do something about it. My peers have been around longer, though, and they know. I take a deep breath and can't help myself.

"The programs kind of suck. They don't tell you what you really need to know, and they often contain outdated content and errors. They don't teach what to do when the truck is late, someone doesn't show, or the POS system breaks down. Frankly, they need to be so much better."

I scan their faces, waiting for a reaction.

Then, Mike exclaims, "Finally! Someone who is willing to be honest with us!"

They all laugh, and I breathe a sigh of relief. I pull a manual off the shelf and show them examples of errors and inconsistencies. I share my ideas, and they take notes. I offer to help them because I believe that great training is the foundation of everything. I tell them that when I was a new manager, I needed much more help, and it could have started with better training.

After thirty minutes, Connie gives me his recognition award for being a leader among my peers and speaking up. Then, they leave.

I immediately dial Sarah, who is still at her restaurant. "They are headed your way. Good luck."

It's over. *All that planning and cleaning for a thirty minute visit. Wonder if it even matters.*

Six months later, I am surprised to get a phone call from Sandi, who works in the Training Department. "Remember me?" she asks.

"Of course, I remember you."

"We are wondering if you want to help us on a project to create job aids for team members."

Without even hearing the details, I enthusiastically say, "Yes!"

Just like that, I am working with Corporate on a project. Every night, Sandi faxes me drafts of the new tools. I mark them up with my edits and fax them back. Here I am, in my restaurant in Chicago, working with Corporate in California on a project to help managers and team members. *The visit mattered. They remembered me.*

■■■ Looking Back ■■■

A few years after the visit from Corporate Taco Bell, I interviewed for a job at the headquarters of Taco Bell in Irvine, California, working in the Training Department. I accepted the position to design training materials for Taco Bell managers across the country. I was sad to leave my Chicago friends, but California? No more Chicago winters? Palm trees and the beach? *Am I dreaming?*

Real leaders show up.

Several months after I moved to the headquarters, I learned more about what had happened on the day they visited my restaurant in Chicago. The Corporate team had met for several hours in the office. It was late, so they decided to visit a few restaurants and then go to a fancy dinner in Chicago. Everyone agreed, except Sandi. Sandi insisted that they visit all the restaurants. She demanded it. "Those restaurant managers have been planning for weeks to see us. They have been waiting all day. We owe it to them to show up."

That is why they arrived so late: because Sandi insisted that they show up.

In my role as Chief Operations Officer, I visited KFC restaurants across the country. I met franchisees, district managers, and team members, and my favorite folks were the restaurant managers. I was one of them. I knew how excited they were to get visitors. I knew how hard they had worked to prepare for me. *I mean, really – me? Who am I?*

It was a big day for them, and, every time, I remembered Sandi. Regardless of how late it was, when the dinner reservation was, or how bad the traffic was, I showed up with full energy and gratitude because that was what Sandi taught me. Real leaders show up.

Note: Sandi Spivey and I went on to become great friends. We walked hundreds of miles together to raise money for breast cancer research. Sandi lived for over two decades with metastatic breast cancer. While working in Human Resources and undergoing dozens of treatments, she became a nationally renowned expert on, and a fierce advocate for, patients battling metastatic breast cancer. In March 2021, after dealing with the disease for two decades, Sandi made her transition. She was a role model in perseverance, fighting for what she believed in, and showing up - always showing up.

Lessons

- **Be positive and honest when giving feedback.** When someone asks you how things can improve, tell the truth. Be solution oriented, but be frank. Your idea may be a game-changer.

- **Say Yes.** Take every advantage to grow yourself. Say yes to projects. Offer to help your company solve a big problem. These opportunities enrich your work life. You gain experience, and you never know when one visit or conversation will change your life.

- **Show up. Do what you say.** If you tell a team that you will be there, then be there full-on for your teams, your peers, your company, and your customers. Even though that event, one-on-one discussion, store visit, or meeting might not mean much to you, your team member is counting down the hours to have the chance to spend time with you.

CONCLUSION: IT'S YOUR TURN

Fall of 2023. Author and Coach,
Louisville, Kentucky

The lessons I learned from managing a drive-thru Taco Bell stayed with me. They shaped my values. I made a conscious decision about the kind of leader I wanted to be. While I was nowhere near perfect, I was always striving to live up to my guiding principles.

The lessons also helped me figure out what was mine to do. Working in the restaurant helped me discover where I excelled, where I struggled, and what brought me the greatest joy. Knowing what is mine to do has helped me remember to find my joy. As Chief Operations Officer of KFC US, I sometimes got tired of endless meetings. They sucked the life out of me. In those times, I went back to what I'm good at: visiting restaurants and talking to restaurant managers! It's mine to do, and it brings me joy!

Though I retired as COO, I still enjoy observing the interaction between leaders and their teams, whether it's at the grocery store, a restaurant, car rental counter, or retail store. I see some managers really struggling.

Recently, I was at a fast-food restaurant and watched the restaurant manager rant at her assistant manager. "You want more closing shifts? You can't even handle the day shift! You want more hours? You need to do a lot better –"

As soon as she was done with him, he went back to the kitchen and yelled at the shift manager, "You need to get that trainee trained!"

I watched the team members give side glances to each other, nervous and fearful. Not surprisingly, I was uncomfortable, and my experience as a customer was terrible.

I've also seen some amazing leaders. A few months ago, I was driving home from a road trip in Indianapolis, and I was hungry. I saw the Taco Bell highway sign and pulled off in Scottsburg, Indiana. I ordered a Crunchwrap Supreme and settled into the dining room to watch the show. In this restaurant, the manager was on a rare break, sitting two tables away from me. The team behind the counter was playful and relaxed. They were productive, but enjoying themselves. Every time a team member came up to ask the manager a question, she would answer them and then say, "Thank you. I love you." Every time!

I had to meet this manager. I walked over and introduced myself as a former Taco Bell RGM writing a book called *Lessons from the Drive-Thru*. I can't imagine how sketchy I sounded. Regardless, Katelyn Phillips introduced herself. We talked for an hour, and I was a fan.

Katelyn started as a team member in 2012, learned to run shifts as a shift manager, was promoted to assistant, and became a restaurant manager in 2020. She describes her two-step philosophy. "First, take care of your employees, and they will take care of you. Second, happy employees mean happy customers."

Let me tell you about Allen Likens. I met Allen through LinkedIn, and I am so impressed with his passion for helping team members. Allen started his career as a dishwasher and is currently an assistant manager. He told me, "I like to teach, coach, and mentor the team to be the best they can be and help them grow to be the leader I am today for their tomorrow."

Allen believes that "you can always find a way through tough times together as a team. Twenty-five sets of eyes are always better than one. If you guide your team through the next storm, your team will guide you through the next several storms, with you overseeing and guiding them on what paths to take. I help them be one percent better every day."

Rebekah Avis is one of the highest-performing managers in KFC. She leads the KFC in Bakersfield, California, one of the busiest restaurants in the country. How does she do it? She takes care of her team, works around their schedules when they need time off, and treats them with respect. Her secret is creating a winning mindset. For her team, it's the Super Bowl or nothing, so people fight to be on her team to be a part of something special.

I'm sure there are leaders like Katelyn, Allen, and Rebekah in every organization. They are the all-stars who have figured out what is theirs to do. My dream is for every leader to unlock their potential to become an all-star. As I said in the introduction, it is my greatest hope that you can use my experience to build your own guiding

You can discover what is yours to do and become the leader no one ever leaves.

principles. You can create an environment where your team members feel loved and appreciated. You can discover what is yours to do and become the leader no one ever leaves.

If enough of us accept this challenge to do what is ours to do and empower our team members, we can change organizations, industries, and society. I'll be watching, cheering you on. You got this.

POST A REVIEW

Hey!

Thanks for taking the time to read my book. I hope you found it useful and entertaining. I have a favor to ask of you.

I'd really appreciate it if you would give a rating wherever you bought the book. Online bookstores promote books that readers are discussing. Your review will create awareness so other frontline leaders can find my book.

It doesn't have to be a long review. Just go to the website where you bought the book, search for my name and the book, and write a few sentences about how it helped you. It would be really cool if you posted a picture of you and your team.

Many thanks for all your support.

Monica Rothgery

SHARE THIS BOOK WITH LEADERS YOU KNOW OR YOUR ENTIRE ORGANIZATION!

If you have found this book valuable and know others who would find it useful, consider buying them a copy as a gift. Special bulk discounts are available if you would like your whole team or organization to benefit from reading this book. Contact Monica@MonicaRothgery.com to inquire.

WOULD YOU LIKE MONICA ROTHGERY TO SPEAK TO YOUR ORGANIZATION?

Book Monica Now!

Monica accepts a limited number of speaking and coaching engagements each year. To learn how you can bring her message to your organization, email

Monica@MonicaRothgery.com or visit
MonicaRothgery.com.

ACKNOWLEDGMENTS

Most acknowledgments end with "last but not least…" and the author mentions her family. Not me. I'm starting with those I love the most. To my beloved wife, Onyxe Antara, who supports me in every endeavor. From sunny California, to big-city living in Bangkok, Thailand, then to the heart of Louisville, you have listened to every story a hundred times. You make me believe in what is possible and help me be the best version of myself. You are the most detailed editor, thoughtful critic, and tireless cheerleader. None of it would be possible without you. I see you.

Dad and Mom, you always made me believe I was special and I could do anything, and now I've written a book! And to Meg, Julie, Paul, John, Rick, and Kati, I am so grateful that we have each other. To Faith, Amelia, Wyatt, Lucy, Carly, Loretta, Jack, and Rex – you can do anything! To JoMama, you always say yes. I appreciate how you support Onyxe and me.

I have a whole lot of people to thank, but I want to start with an organization, the one where I spent my entire career – Yum! Brands – for providing me with opportunities for thirty years to grow as a leader. I worked with brilliant and passionate leaders and was never far from a restaurant. I mean, who doesn't like tacos, pizza, and fried chicken? I worked for all three brands and often get asked which is my favorite. Love the one you're with! Grateful to Yum!

To my team in Thailand, you changed my life, and I will remember you forever. รักคุณมาก มาก – rak khun maak maak. To my teams at Taco Bell and KFC, I am humbled to have worked with you and proud of our work and the leaders you became. To my peers at Taco Bell and my posse at KFC, you are the reason I stayed thirty years. Best in class! To KFC franchisees: I am incredibly grateful for your support when I was COO. You all are the best. Now, buy my book!

Writing this book didn't take an army of researchers or writers. It was just me, my memories, and my Macbook. But publishing this book and making it worthy of a reader – that took some help. I want to thank everyone who helped me bring this collection of stories to life. Greg Creed, I cried when I read the foreword. You are one of a kind! Honored to call you a mentor and privileged to call you a friend. Marci Dubois, you are one class act, and your contribution to this book was perfection. Cathy Fyock, you are the book coach that I needed. Yes! Authors have the power to change the world, one word at a time. Thanks to my editorial board – Cathy Fyock, Kathy Gosser, Kristin Kaiser, Ferril Onyett, Katelyn Phillips, and Scott Shultz – what a selfless, generous act. You made my good book a great book.

To Everett O'Keefe and the team at Ignite Press: You made publishing a book easy. From day one, I knew I was in good hands. Owen Sammarone, you taught me how to talk about the book so it gets into the hands of those who need it.

I have always been a writer, but now I am an author, speaker, and branded expert, thanks to a whole bunch of friends who showed up to help. Sandy Ko, you were the first to give me a chance to share my message. You opened the door. BlackBird Writers group, you inspire me. Laura Munson, words can't express the depth of my gratitude. You were the first to read *Lessons from the Drive-Thru*, and you made me believe it was something special. The Haven Writing Retreat was a turning point. To my speaker mentors: Shep Hyken, Dan Thurmon, Scott Greenberg, and Justin Patton, you are selfless in your time and advice in teaching me to take what I know and share it with others from the stage. To Gab and Brian Bosché, founders of The Purpose Company, this is what your vision looks like when you help people like me fulfill their purpose.

The stories in the book happened over thirty years ago, as I remember them today. I changed names and genders where appropriate, but all were real people who walked through those experiences with me. My assistant managers, Johnny and Daryl, were two of the best, and both went on to have careers in the industry. Phil and Paul Stachewicz, and all the managers I worked with back in Chicago, survived OOF and proved that every restaurant needs a leader.

To Khalil, Katelyn, Allen, Rebekah, and all of you leaders leading from the frontline: This book is for you. Know that I believe in you and your ability to change lives.

ABOUT THE AUTHOR

Monica Rothgery started her career as a manager for Taco Bell. Twenty-five years later, she was the first woman to become Chief Operations Officer for KFC in the United States. She was also the first LGBTQ leader promoted to the C-Suite at Yum! Brands, one of the largest restaurant companies in the world. A speaker and coach, Monica helps leaders – especially women – discover their inner power and realize their potential to change lives. Monica lives in Louisville, Kentucky, with her wife, Onyxe, and their fur babies, Louis and Skye.

Monica can be reached at: MonicaRothgery.com